THE LETTERS OF JOHN

THE GOD OF LIGHT, LOVE, AND LIFE

THE LETTERS OF JOHN

THE GOD OF LIGHT, LOVE, AND LIFE

Frazer Discipleship

What is Frazer 365?

Frazer 365 is one church's attempt to touch every member every day with the Word of God. Acts 2:46 teaches that the early church met **"day by day, attending the temple together."** While most members cannot get to our campus every day, we can still study His Word daily together in community. We believe that God works in miraculous ways when every member studies the same Scripture each day. We have also discovered that an expositional approach to the study of Scripture keeps us from skipping the difficult sections and provides us the whole counsel of God's Word.

At Frazer, we believe that the Word of God **"is living and active."** (Hebrews 4:12a)

The Bible is alive with God's truth, and it activates our spiritual growth. Proper application to our daily lives works to help us follow His will.

At Frazer, we believe that the Word of God is **"sharper than any two-edged sword, piercing to the division of soul and of spirit, of joints and of marrow."** (Hebrews 4:12b)

The Bible properly divided, penetrates our lives, and reveals the core of who we are meant to be in Christ. Scripture clearly cuts to the heart of God's purpose and plan for the life He has given us. At times, it painfully points out the sin in our lives.

At Frazer, we believe that the Word of God discerns **"the thoughts and intentions of the heart."** (Hebrews 4:12c)

The Holy Spirit speaks to us through God's Word and uncovers our thoughts and intentions. Scripture points out wrong thinking and misdirected motives and guides us back to a godly mindset, unselfish attitude, and a serving spirit.

At Frazer, we believe that: **"All Scripture is breathed out by God and profitable for teaching, for reproof, for correction, and for training in righteousness, that the man of God may be complete, equipped for every good work."** (2 Timothy 3:16-17)

At Frazer, we believe that His Word is **"a lamp to my feet."** (Psalm 119:105a)

Godly Wisdom comes from His Word. Scripture shines a light on God's will so you can see where He wants your next steps to be.

At Frazer, we believe that His Word is **"a light to my path."** (Psalm 119:105b)

As you commit to **Frazer 365**, may His Word illuminate your path as you take daily steps of faith in your journey with Him.

Table of Contents

The Letters of John

Introduction

Today, we embark on a 56-day journey through **The Letters of John**. May this journey bring you into a stronger fellowship with the God of light, love, and life.

John Phillips gives incredible wisdom to introduce a study of these three letters:

> John wrote for the third generation. Peter and Paul, James and Jude all wrote for the first and second generations of believers. John, however, as a first-generation apostle, passed over two generations to write for an increasingly apostate third generation.
>
> For by its third generation, every movement of God needs a fresh touch of the Holy Spirit. The first generation is motivated by *conviction*; great truths have been grasped, and those who have espoused them have a compulsion to spread those truths abroad. They will dare all and die for them. The second generation inherits these truths, but the conviction softens into a *belief*. They believe the truths they have been taught; they debate them, defend them, and disseminate them, but the fire and passion have gone. By the third generation, the belief becomes an *opinion*. The third generation will trade first-generation truth, dilute it, change it, accept counterfeits, and make room for error. And that's why John wrote for the third generation—the third generation needed a fresh revival.[1]

Who wrote them?

These three letters are widely attributed to John, the beloved disciple of Jesus who wrote the fourth Gospel. Every Greek and Latin church father accepted these epistles as authored by John. The style and vocabulary of the letters are so strikingly similar to those of John's Gospel that most scholars agree that the same author wrote all four books.

When were they written?

Bruce Wilkinson and Kenneth Boa, in *Talk thru the Bible*, give the following discussion on the date of writings for 1 John:

> In Acts 8:14, John is associated with "the apostles who were at Jerusalem," and Paul calls him one of the "pillars" of the Jerusalem church in Galatians 2:9. Apart from Revelation 1, the New Testament is silent about his later years, but early Christian tradition uniformly tells us that he left Jerusalem (probably not long before its destruction in 70 AD) and that he ministered in and around Ephesus. The seven churches in the Roman province of Asia, mentioned in Revelation 2 and 3, were evidently a part of this ministry. Although there is no address in First John, it is likely that the apostle directed this epistle to the Asian churches that were within the realm of his oversight.
>
> The believers in these congregations were well established in Christian truth, and John wrote to them not as novices but as brethren grounded in apostolic doctrine (2:7, 18–27; 3:11). The apostle does not mention his own affairs, but his use of such terms of address

as "beloved" and "my little children" gives this letter a personal touch that reveals his close relationship to the original recipients. First John was probably written in Ephesus after the Gospel of John, but the date cannot be fixed with certainty. No persecution is mentioned, suggesting a date prior to 95 AD when persecution broke out during the end of Domitian's reign (81–96 AD).[2]

Wilkinson goes on to date the writings of the second and third letters of John to approximately 90 AD.

What was the purpose?

It appears by the language found in these letters, that John wrote to a mainly Jewish audience that had recently gone through a crisis. This is what motivated him to write these letters. In 1 John 2:18-23 and 4:1-3, John describes this group as having left the church and denied Jesus as the Son of God. John acknowledges that this group has also caused hostility toward those who had stayed faithful to Christ (1 John 3:4-10). The second and third letters of John clearly addressed this conflict. 2 John was a warning to a specific house church full of deceivers who had denied Jesus. 3 John was written to Gaius, who is a member of another house church. John told Gaius to welcome the genuine missionaries who were about to come to his church. John wrote to Gaius with these instructions because the leader of this house church, Diotrephes, was rejecting anyone associated with John. So these letters give us a picture of the conflict and heresy that John battled within these churches.

Curtis Vaughan describes heresy that John is combatting when he writes the following about 1 John:

It is a crisis letter, having been written to stem the tide of a deadly doctrinal error that threatened to destroy the fellowship of the churches of Asia. This controversy is reflected in nearly every verse of the letter, but its distinctive features are most clearly delineated in 2:18–28 and 4:1–6. It is universally agreed that the error in question was some form of Gnosticism, a quasi-philosophical movement that had its beginnings in the latter part of the first Christian century and came to full flower in the middle of the second century.

Gnosticism was essentially a combination of oriental mysticism and Greek philosophy. Eventually, it took on just enough of Christianity to make it a formidable foe to the faith. John considered it a counterfeit Christianity . . .[3]

In view of this conflict, John writes about true Christian love. In fact, no other book in the New Testament speaks about love more than 1 John. Thus, John is writing these letters so even through a crisis, the churches in Asia will show the love of Christ to one another.

Charles Swindoll gives great insight into John's purpose for writing these letters:

In the twilight of his long life, the apostle John gathered his thoughts, surveyed the landscape of the world around him, and then sat down with parchment and ink to sum up his final words to the churches.

So much had changed since he had walked with Jesus as one of the original Twelve. Those brief but impactful three-plus years John spent with Jesus were followed by six long and painful decades. Erosion had set into the life of the church. In many places, the newness of fresh

4

faith had begun to wane now that the church was in the hands of second - and third-generation Christians. A subtle, lethargic boredom had replaced the excitement modeled by those early followers of Jesus. The initial thrill had subsided, the bright flame of devotion reduced to a flicker.

In a setting like that, the subtle seeds of heresy are easily sown and rapidly grown. Cults feed off complacent churches, where ho-hum indifference replaces dynamic enthusiasm. Also, over the course of time, core values like truth, love, and hospitality can begin to be compromised, misdirected, and abused. Tragically, these scenarios were playing out in the church of John's day—and that's precisely what led him to write these letters.

When he wrote the letter known today as 1st John, it's likely that the aged apostle had more years behind him than he had months ahead of him. He was probably somewhere between 88 and 93 years of age. Let's just call him a 90-year-old man. Isn't it remarkable that a man at that age was so in touch with his times? In fact, I would argue that *because* of his age, he saw more clearly than ever. And that's what troubled him enough to write this letter.

Here, nearing the end of his life, with clarity of perspective and singularity of purpose, the Lord's "beloved disciple" sought to revive the faith, love, and hope of his younger readers. He hoped to encourage them to renew an authentic, contagious walk with Christ. And his message of right living in a wrong world is as relevant today as it was then.[4]

Why are they important?

The Letters of John describe how believers are to walk in true fellowship with God. God is light, so those who follow Christ must live in light, not in darkness. God is love, so His children must walk in love. God is life, so those who fellowship with God display a fulfilled life.

In the letters, John states that the Holy Spirit is Who enables a believer to live an obedient Christian life. The writings connect the believer's love for Christ with an active love for their brothers and sisters in Christ. So, a believer's walk connects to their daily life and ties into how they treat others.

Day One

The Letters of John

An Intimate Fellowship with God

First John is a book about love. Another word for love is
the word intimacy. If you have a growing relationship with
someone, you are becoming more and more intimate with
them. You are becoming closer and closer.
David Anderson[1]

Text: 1 John 1:1

[1] That which was from the beginning, which we have heard,
which we have seen with our eyes, which we looked upon
and have touched with our hands, concerning the word of life.

Thoughts:

In the beginning, Adam and Eve had a perfect relationship
with God. Before the fall, they were in paradise with the God of
all creation. However, sin changed everything. The sin nature in
our lives attacks true love and intimacy.

David Anderson shares the following insight:

One of those blocks to intimacy lies at the very core
of the sin nature. It is selfishness. Selfishness focuses on
getting, not giving. Love, by definition, is giving, but the
sin nature grabs and gets. People often confuse love and
lust, but the main difference between the two is selfishness. Love asks, "How can I meet your needs?" whereas

lust asks, "How can you meet mine?" So the sin nature works against intimacy because it is selfish.

But there is something else contained in the sin nature which is a block to intimacy, and that's fear. Fear is one of the greatest stumbling blocks to opening up. You can't be intimate with someone if you don't open up. You can't be close to someone if you don't share the things close to you. But we are afraid to do that. . . .

This fear of rejection keeps us from opening up and getting close. But there is good news. God has given us 1 John to show how to have intimacy after the fall, to show how we can have our most fundamental need for love met even though there is sin in the world, in the universe, and resident within us. That's why 1 John was written.[2]

God desires an intimate relationship with His children. He wants you to know Him and be known by Him. When you read the first verse of 1 John, you can't miss John's assertion that God is real and personal. John had a personal relationship with God and intimate fellowship with Him.

Notice the progression in the personal encounter John had with God found in 1 John 1:1: heard, seen, looked upon, and touched. John had heard God speak. The beloved disciple had seen Jesus with his own eyes and intently gazed at Him. He had even physically touched Jesus with his own hands. A relationship with God is not just a neat concept, it is an amazing reality. And genuine fellowship with God is not just for the spiritual elite, but for all of God's children.

Questions:

1. What specifically in your sinful nature hinders your fellowship with God?

2. In what ways are you growing closer to Jesus?

3. What is the distinction between having a permanent relationship with God and having intimate fellowship with Him?

Day Two

The Letters of John

The Power of a Witness

Yes, let God be the Judge.
Your job today is to be a witness.
Warren Wiersbe [1]

Text: 1 John 1:2-3
[2] the life was made manifest, and we have seen it, and testify to it and proclaim to you the eternal life, which was with the Father and was made manifest to us – [3] that which we have seen and heard we proclaim also to you, so that you too may have fellowship with us; and indeed our fellowship is with the Father and with his Son Jesus Christ.

Thoughts:
   John continues his opening by stressing his personal experience with Jesus Christ. Because of John's close relationship with Jesus, he was careful not to make light of the incredible privilege of knowing Him. John would not dare understate the honor he had in genuine fellowship with almighty God:

> . . . can we actually share with someone else about a
> God we do not understand or tell others about a God we
> have not experienced?

Our understanding and our experience are not the end of our witness about God, but they must be the beginning of our witness about God. We cannot share what we do not understand or have not experienced.

John knew that. Consequently, as he began the book we know as 1 John, he rooted his opening words in the experience he had shared with Jesus and the understanding that had developed from that experience.[2]

In 1 John 1:2, John described Jesus as eternal life sent from God the Father. Twice John uses the word "manifest" to describe how Jesus was made known to him. The Greek word for "manifest" comes from another New Testament word that means "light." This word "manifest" means "to illumine in order to make visible." Therefore, God made Jesus clearly visible to John so that he could personally fellowship with Him.

Charles Swindoll points out that 1 John 1:1-3 is one single sentence in the original language of the New Testament. Swindoll also notes that the main verb doesn't appear until verse 3 with the words, "we proclaim." Thus, the main emphasis of the first few verses of 1 John is John telling his readers what he had seen and heard to impact the fellowship others had with one another, and to influence the fellowship other people had with Jesus. So, John's proclamation of Jesus as "The Word of Life" resulted in true fellowship.

Questions:

1. In today's scripture, what is the significance of John referring to Jesus as "the life" and "eternal life"?

2. John also announced what he had "seen and heard" in today's passage. In your relationship with Jesus, what have you "seen and heard" that needs to be your witness for Jesus to others?

3. How can your witness impact the fellowship of other believers and, at the same time, enhance your own fellowship with Jesus?

Day Three

The Letters of John

Complete Joy

The truest, purest joy flows from a discovery of Jesus Christ.
He is the hidden treasure that gives joy to the finder.
Robert Murray McCheyne[1]

Text: 1 John 1:4
[4] And we are writing these things so that our joy may be complete.

Thoughts:

John writes about experiencing true fellowship with Jesus Christ so that his readers will find complete joy. The word complete that John uses to describe joy in 1 John 1:4 means "to be full" or "to fill to capacity." John knows that writing about authentic fellowship through a real relationship with Jesus leads to complete joy.

The authors of the *Life Application Bible Commentary* on 1 John made the following connection between proclamation, fellowship, and joy:

John wrote this letter to encourage the readers' participation in both the fellowship and the joy that he (John) and the other believers were experiencing. Proclamation produces fellowship; fellowship produces joy. John's joy would be complete if his read-

13

ers remained in the fellowship and did not wander off into false teaching. John, caretaker of the churches and "spiritual father" to many of the believers in and around Ephesus, would only be able to experience "complete joy" if his "children" were experiencing the blessings of fellowship with one another and with God.[2]

A growing relationship with Jesus stems from the unending reciprocal effect of this cycle of joy. John proclaimed what he had seen and heard. His witness led to deeper fellowship. That deeper fellowship with Jesus resulted in more joy. When you are filled to capacity with the joy of Jesus, you can't help but share it.

Joy was a recurring theme with Jesus and John often wrote about it. Notice the following Scriptures:

John 15:11 (ESV)

[11] These things I have spoken to you, that my joy may be in you, and that your joy may be full.

John 16:22-24 (ESV)

[22] So also you have sorrow now, but I will see you again, and your hearts will rejoice, and no one will take your joy from you. [23] In that day you will ask nothing of me. Truly, truly, I say to you, whatever you ask of the Father in my name, he will give it to you. [24] Until now you have asked nothing in my name. Ask, and you will receive, that your joy may be full.

John 17:13 (ESV)

[13] But now I am coming to you, and these things I speak in the world, that they may have my joy fulfilled in themselves.

Jesus wants you to experience complete joy. He said that if you ask for joy, you will receive full joy. One of God's purposes for your life is that His joy will be fulfilled in you.

Questions:

1. Is your joy full? Why or why not?

2. Read the following quote by David Martyn Lloyd–Jones:

> He is our joy and our happiness, even as He is our peace. He is life, He is everything. Place at the center the only One who has a right to be there, the Lord of Glory, who so loved you that He went to the Cross and bore the punishment and the shame of your sins and died for you. Seek Him, seek His face, and all other things shall be added unto you.[3]

As you concentrate on these truths about your fellowship with God, what thoughts come to your mind?

3. You read the following quote from the *Life Application Bible Commentary*:

"Proclamation produces fellowship;
fellowship produces joy."

Where is your weakest link in this chain of events?
What needs to take place in your life regularly so that you can experience joy fully?

Day Four

The Letters of John

God is Light

Light represents God's presence and power.
David A. Case and David W. Holdren[1]

Text: 1 John 1:5
⁵ This is the message we have heard from him and proclaim to you, that God is light, and in him is no darkness at all.

Thoughts:
The message that John announced was simple, yet profound. God is light. In Him, there is no darkness. Light represents God's presence and His power.

Today, think about a few characteristics of light that enhance our understanding of who God is.

First, light demonstrates. Light can't help but shine. Light validates that it is light by shining into the darkness. In the same way, God cannot help but shine. Because He is the Light, He shines into the darkness.

John recorded the following declaration from Jesus in John 8:12:

¹² Again Jesus spoke to them, saying, "I am the light of the world. Whoever follows me will not walk in darkness, but will have the light of life."

As John wrote his first letter, I believe that he vividly remembered these words from Jesus. After John wrote Jesus' words, "I am the light of the world," he wrote, "God is light, and in Him is no darkness at all."

Jesus is light within His very nature. As believers, we receive light from Christ. The world is meant to see Jesus in us. We are to demonstrate who Jesus is by who we are and what we say. One main reason lost people haven't trusted Jesus for salvation is that there are so few Christians who demonstrate what it is to know and serve Jesus.

I heard about a little boy who was taken by his mother to see a famous cathedral. On the windows were the pictures of various Christians. As he watched the sunbeams shining through the stained-glass windows, he asked his mother, "Who are those people on the windows?" She said, "They're saints." The little boy looked at the windows and said, "Well, now I know what saints are. They are people who let the light shine through."

Light also illuminates. The purpose of light is to shine and to be seen. If we truly are the light, it cannot be hidden. Someone once said, "There is no such thing as secret discipleship. If you are lit, you will shine."

Light points the way in darkness, and it warns people of danger. When you travel at night, you turn on your vehicle's headlights. Your lights give you enough illumination to see the road in front of you. If there is approaching danger because of road construction, there are flashing lights in front of you to warn you. In the same way, Jesus is the light. As the light, He points the way and signals the world of danger that lies ahead.

As followers of Christ, we are to shine His light to point others to Jesus, who is the Way. We also have God's Word as a lamp unto our feet and a light unto our path to warn people of the dangers ahead. (See Psalm 119:105.)

We have people all around us who are lost in the darkness of this world and do not know the light of Christ. If they die without Christ, they will be separated from Him forever. These people are in grave danger unless they see the illuminated light of Jesus.

Questions:

1. What other characteristics of light can you list that describe who God is as "the Light"?

2. In what ways does your light demonstrate and validate that you have received the light of Christ?

3. What specifically can you do to shine His light to point the way in darkness and warn others of danger?

Day Five

The Letters of John

Walk in the Light

Words which do not give the light of Christ
increase the darkness.
Mother Teresa[1]

Text: 1 John 1:6-7
[6] If we say we have fellowship with him while we walk in darkness, we lie and do not practice the truth. [7] But if we walk in the
light, as he is in the light, we have fellowship with one another,
and the blood of Jesus his Son cleanses us from all sin.

Thoughts:
　　Paul Harvey's *The Rest of the Story* contained some of the
greatest stories ever told outside of God's Word. The following
story, Paul Harvey simply entitled "The Light Show":

> On the night of April 14, the ocean liner *Californian*
> had progressed to within fifteen hundred miles of her
> destination, Boston Harbor. It was midnight and Second
> Officer Herbert Stone, and his apprentice, were star-
> ing through their binoculars toward the black horizon.
> The apprentice had sighted a steamer in the distance.
> He could make out the ship's masthead light, her red
> light, and a glare of white lights on her afterdeck. The
> two tried to communicate with the steamer using the

Californian's Morse Lamp. A bright beacon is flashed, no answer from the steamer. The apprentice turned in for the night. Officer Stone remained, and saw a white flash of light in the sky coming from over the area of the distant steamer. He watched as four more white flashes, like skyrockets bursting in the heavens, shot forth. Stone notified the ship's captain. The Captain asked if the flashes appeared to be company signals. Stone cannot say for sure. Then Stone tried to communicate through the Morse lamp once more. Still no answer from the steamer. Stone, through his binoculars, saw three more white flashes in the continuing light show, but now his attention was drawn to the cabin lights. They seemed to be disappearing as though the steamer was sailing away. At 1:40 A.M., Stone saw the eighth and last white flash in the night sky.

It was not until 4:00 A.M. that the *Californian* discovered the meaning of the light show. Neither the Captain nor the Second Officer aboard the *Californian* had interpreted the white skyrockets as cause for alarm. It was a matter of coincidence that they had been seen in the first place. For earlier that night, the night of April 14, the *Californian* had reversed engines as a precautionary measure, halted in her course by an immense field of oceanic ice. That stop had provided the *Californian* with a ringside seat for an unimaginable drama. The distant steamer had intended those rocket flares as distress signals, and the *Californian,* only nine miles away - might have rushed to her aid. Except for one thing. The steamer was sending other distress calls – by radio. And the *Californian* was well within range of those messages. But her radio operator was asleep. The *Californian's* rookie radio operator, fresh from training school - was

21

fast asleep in his cabin. And that night the ship's Second Officer, from his vantage point on the bridge, unwittingly watched the sinking of the *Titanic!*[2]

In the same way, the world around us is drowning in a sea of sin. The world is decaying all around us. And God is our Captain. As Christians, we are all second officers. And we are unknowingly and sometimes willingly ignoring the distress signals all around us. The world is lost in sin. Jesus calls us to "walk in the light, as he is in the light." If we walk in the light, we will "have fellowship with one another, and the blood of Jesus His Son cleanses us from all sin."

Dr. James Stewart, a great British preacher, once said: "The greatest threat to Christianity is Christians trying to sneak into heaven incognito without ever sharing their faith, without ever living out the Christian life, without ever becoming involved in the most significant work God is doing on planet earth."

John proclaimed the message that God is light. He also challenged all believers to walk in the light.

Questions:

1. Carefully meditate on 1 John 1:6:

> [6] If we say we have fellowship with him while we walk in darkness, we lie and do not practice the truth.

Are there any areas of your life where your talk does not match up with your walk? Confess them to God and repent of your actions. Ask God to help you to walk in the light.

2. In what specific ways are you walking in the light of Christ?

3. Matthew 5:14-16 records the following challenge from Jesus:

> [14] "You are the light of the world. A city set on a hill cannot be hidden. [15] Nor do people light a lamp and put it under a basket, but on a stand, and it gives light to all in the house. [16] In the same way, let your light shine before others, so that they may see your good works and give glory to your Father who is in heaven."

How does this challenge connect with 1 John 1:6-7?

Day Six

The Letters of John

He is Faithful to Forgive

People who conceal their sins will not prosper,
but if they confess and turn from them,
they will receive mercy.
Proverbs 28:13 (NLT)

Text: 1 John 1:8-9

⁸ If we say we have no sin, we deceive ourselves, and the truth is not in us. ⁹ If we confess our sins, he is faithful and just to forgive us our sins and to cleanse us from all unrighteousness.

Thoughts:

We have two choices when it comes to the sin in our lives. We can lie and say we don't have any sin to confess. Or we can confess our sin to God. If we choose to deny it, we cannot be cleansed from it. If we confess it, God is faithful to forgive us. Either you must live with your sin daily, or you can find freedom through God's forgiveness.

1 John 1:9 is a very popular Scripture among Christians. Those of us who have grown up in church memorized this verse early in our lives. Even though I knew of this verse, I never studied it intently until just a few years ago. I felt the Holy Spirit nudge me to look up the verbs in this verse in the original language. What I discovered has greatly impacted my

spiritual journey ever since.

The verb "confess" is in the present active tense. This means that every day, we need to actively confess our sins. Confession should be the practice of every believer. So, confession is a present-tense decision.

There are two more verbs in 1 John 1:9. "Forgive us" and "cleanse us." This is God's part. We confess and God forgives and cleanses. The interesting fact about those two verbs is that they are both in the *aorist* tense. This tense in the Greek language shows past completed action.

How do we apply this Scripture and these verb tenses to our spiritual journey? We confess our sin daily. God puts it in the past, and once and for all, forgiveness is completed. We confess it every single day; God forgives it and forgets it.

You see, God didn't send Jesus to die on the cross so that you could live every single day like a spiritual pity party. "I wish I hadn't done this, and I wish I hadn't done that." No! God sent Jesus Christ His Son not just to get us to Heaven one day, but to give us abundant life today! We can live daily in the forgiveness that God provides. Because of the grace of God, He sees your confessed sin as completely cleansed. God doesn't bring it back up. When you confess it, God replaces your guilt with His grace. He wipes your slate clean so that you can be what He called you to be!

At this moment, you are either living in your sin or forgiven of your sin. Either you are living in guilt, and you find yourself in a prison of your own making because you will not confess your sins to God, or you are living in God's forgiveness because God is faithful to forgive what you have confessed. If you are still holding yourself hostage to your own sins, God wants to set you free.

Our Heavenly Father sees it all. He hears everything you confess and knows everything you are not willing to confess. You are letting the devil enslave you if you will not confess your sins to God. By your refusal to admit your sins, you are doing the devil's chores. Choose instead the God who sees it all, knows it all, and can forgive everything you have done.

Questions:

1. What sins are you currently not confessing? What reason do you have not to confess them to God?

2. In your past journey with Jesus, how has unconfessed sin hindered your spiritual growth?

3. How can you focus daily on confession and repentance so that God can daily renew your soul?

Day Seven

The Letters of John

Don't Make a Liar Out of The Lord

¹⁰ Whoever believes in the Son of God
has the testimony in himself.
Whoever does not believe God has made him a liar,
because he has not believed in the testimony
that God has borne concerning his Son.
1 John 5:10 (ESV)

Text: 1 John 1:10
¹⁰ If we say we have not sinned, we make him a liar, and his word is not in us.

Thoughts:

In 1 John, there are two references to making God a liar: 1 John 1:10 and 1 John 5:10. In the first, we make God out to be a liar when we claim we have not sinned. If we say we have no sin in our lives, we are liars. If we deny ever sinning in our lives, then we suggest that God is lying about our situation. In 1 John 5:10, we make God out to be a liar when we do not believe in Him. God testified to us about His Son. If we do not believe in His testimony concerning Jesus, we infer that God is a liar.

These two verses have serious implications. John tells us in his Gospel that Jesus is the way, the truth, and the life (see John 14:6). Since God is the truth, He cannot lie. Just as God is light

27

and there is no darkness in Him; God is truth and there is no dishonesty in Him.

When a sinner denies sinning, he makes God out to be a liar because God's entire redemption plan is based on the fact that we have all sinned and fallen short of His glory. To claim that we are free of sin is to allege God's declaration that all have sinned to be a complete lie. If sin is not our fundamental problem, then the Good News of the Gospel is meaningless. If we don't have a sin problem, then God sent His only Son to die for no reason.

The great expositor John Phillips explains the significance of John's statement in 1 John 1:10 by taking us to the book of Romans. Phillips' words are enlightening and convicting:

> God has repeatedly told us in His Word about our sinful condition, and what could be more wicked than to call God a liar? In Romans 1-3 and similar passages, the Holy Spirit thoroughly exposes the sinfulness of the human race. The opening chapters of Romans set before us a court case in which the Holy Spirit acts as the prosecutor of the human race.
>
> All that deceit and wickedness is proved when a person says that he or she has no sin. Such people prove themselves to be wicked by calling God a liar. "His Word is not in them," John says. Such people refuse to believe the Bible and deny the Holy Spirit's thoroughgoing exposure of the corruption, crookedness, and criminality of unregenerate human behavior. The first great work of the Holy Spirit in a human heart, after all, is to convict us of "sin, and of righteousness, and judgment" (John 16:8–11) – of the nature of sin, the need for righteousness, and the nearness of judgment. The person who says he or she

has no sin is evidently a person in whose heart the Holy Spirit has not done even His initial work.[1]

Questions:

1. Has it ever occurred to you that by denying your sin, you are calling God a liar? How does this truth hit home in your heart?

2. Denying sin is a result of an inability to trust God. How can you take Him at His Word so that you can see yourself for who you truly are? How does admitting your true self lead to finding all that God has for you?

3. What did you learn from the comments from John Phillips in today's devotion?

4. In light of John 16:8-11, Phillips said:

> "The person who says he or she has no sin is evidently a person in whose heart the Holy Spirit has not done even His initial work."

What are your thoughts on these very strong words?

Day Eight

The Letters of John

The Lord is Our Lawyer

O Lord, you are my Lawyer! Plead my case!
For You have redeemed my life.
Lamentations 3:58 (TLB)

Text: 1 John 2:1

¹ My little children, I am writing these things to you so that you may not sin. But if anyone does sin, we have an advocate with the Father, Jesus Christ the righteous.

Thoughts:

John reminds us that God has the power to help us live the victorious Christian life. The apostle was writing his letter so that we would know that continual sin should not be the lifestyle of a follower of Jesus Christ. Yet John knows that we will have a sinful nature until we reach Heaven. So the beloved disciple gives us the great news for when we do sin: "We have an advocate with the Father, Jesus Christ the righteous."

The word "advocate" is the Greek word *paraclete*. This word is found only five times in the New Testament, and each occurrence is in the writings of the apostle John. This word is found four times in the Gospel of John and refers to the Holy Spirit as our Helper (John 14:16; 14:26; 15:26; and 16:7). *Paraclete* is found only once in John's letters (1 John 2:1). In today's verse, the word refers personally to Jesus Christ. Every time the word *paraclete* is found in Scripture, it refers to the Holy Spirit or to Jesus Christ.

The word *paraclete* is a compound word, which means it comes from two separate Greek words. One word is *para*, which means "from close beside" and the other is *kaleo*, which means "to make a call." Therefore, a *paraclete* is a legal advocate who makes the right judgment call because he is close enough to the situation.

1 John 2:1 teaches us that when we sin, Jesus comes alongside us as our Helper and Advocate. Christ is always with us and ready to defend us in our time of need. If you were falsely accused of a crime and had to appear in court, you would want the best attorney money could buy. We are all guilty of sin. When the Devil accuses us and takes us before the courtroom of life, we have the best Attorney of all, the Lord Jesus Christ. It cost Jesus His life to represent you before the Father, but He is your Attorney free of charge! He is the perfect Lawyer who has never lost a case. He perfectly fulfilled the law with His life and death, and He mightily represents you with His resurrection power.

When Jesus represents you and I, none of us is innocent. We are all guilty because we have all sinned. So Jesus has never had an innocent client. Jesus pleads with the Judge, not based on our good works or innocence, but based on what He has done for us. John refers to Jesus as "the righteous." Jesus lived a sinless life and died in our place. Therefore, Christ is our righteousness and died as our sacrifice. And on top of all of that, He knows the Judge intimately! The Judge is His Father. Our Lord is our Lawyer who always gains the acquittal for those who trust in Him.

Questions:

1. How would you feel standing guilty before God without Jesus as your defense attorney? How do you think your trial would go?

2. What does it mean to you personally that Jesus defends you before the Father?

3. How can you strive to live victoriously over temptation while remaining thankful that Jesus is your Lawyer when you fail?

Day Nine

The Letters of John

Propitiation – Big Word / Huge Implications

Christ is our Attorney and His portfolio is His propitiation. He stands before His Father in Heaven, and every time we sin, He doesn't make a new propitiation. He doesn't die again and again. Instead, He opens His portfolio and lays the exhibit of Good Friday on the bench before the Judge. Photographs of the crown of thorns, the lashing, the mocking soldiers, the agonies of the cross, and the final cry of victory: It is Finished.

John Piper[1]

Text: 1 John 2:2

[2] He is the propitiation for our sins, and not for ours only but also for the sins of the whole world.

Thoughts:

1 John 2:2 connects with what John later recorded in 1 John 4:10: "In this is love, not that we have loved God but that he loved us and sent His Son to be the propitiation for our sins." The word "propitiation" only occurs four times in Scripture. The two times in 1 John, in Romans 3:25, and in Hebrews 2:17.

Sometimes, preachers can use big words that no one understands. At times, writers do the same thing. John used this big word because it has huge implications in the life of a Christ-follower.

What does it mean that Jesus is our propitiation? Let's go to Rod Mattoon's work, *Treasures from First … Second … Third John*, for wisdom behind the meaning of this great word:

In the New Testament, propitiation refers to the work of God, not the work of men. Men did good works to appease the pagan gods in Greek culture. They wanted to buy off god's anger and purchase his love. We, however, are incapable of satisfying the justice of God. The only acceptable appeasement is made by God Himself.

The Greek word for "propitiation" is *hilasterion*. It comes from the Greek word for sacrifice, *hilasmos*. This root word for sacrifice means "to atone or make payment for." Jesus Christ is the atoning sacrifice for our sins. The word propitiation, *hilasterion*, is a reference to the "mercy seat" in the Jewish Temple. Each year, on the Day of Atonement, the High Priest would sprinkle the blood of the sacrifice on the mercy seat on top of the Ark of the Covenant. He would do this to atone for the sins of the people. The blood could not take away the sin. It could only cover it until the time when Christ would come and purchase a salvation for us that would be totally complete. This is what Jesus did for us. In Heaven, Jesus sprinkled His blood in the presence of God the Father.

Through the blood of Jesus Christ, we have atonement or covering for our sins when we put our faith in Him. Our sins are covered by the blood of Christ. God the Father sees the blood of Christ when He looks at the sinner saved by His grace. The death of Christ was the final and sufficient payment for eternal life. Yet, you must accept His payment. Nothing else such as good works, religious deeds, etc., is sufficient payment for our sins. The blood of Christ is your spiritual protection.

Jesus is our mercy seat. He is our propitiation and secures us from the judgment of God when we put our faith in Him. Our security from judgment is found in Him, and Him alone. In a way, like the cherubim, He protects the way to Heaven by being the only way there. There is no other access to Heaven except through Him.[3]

Out of His great love for us, Jesus paid the penalty of our sin by shedding His blood on the cross (1 John 4:10). Because He took our place and paid for our sins, He is our defense attorney before the Father and the atoning sacrifice for our sins (1 John 2:1-2). We have an incredible Savior who loves us, pays our penalty, and defends us.

Questions:

1. How does Romans 3:23-25 add to your understanding of the biblical concept of propitiation?

Romans 3:23-25 (ESV)
[23] for all have sinned and fall short of the glory of God, [24] and are justified by his grace as a gift, through the redemption that is in Christ Jesus, [25] whom God put forward as a propitiation by his blood, to be received by faith. This was to show God's righteousness, because in his divine forbearance he had passed over former sins.

2. What does Hebrews 2:17 teach you about Jesus as your pro-pitiation?

Hebrews 2:17 (ESV)
    ¹⁷ Therefore he had to be made like his brothers in every respect, so that he might become a merciful and faithful high priest in the service of God, to make propitiation for the sins of the people.

3. How can this big word with huge implications – propitiation – encourage you to be closer to Christ?

Day Ten

The Letters of John

Knowing that You Know Him

What were we made for? To know God.
What aim should we have in life? To know God.
What is the eternal life that Jesus gives? To know God.
What is the best thing in life? To know God.
What in humans gives God the most pleasure?
Knowledge of Himself.
J. I. Packer

Once you become aware that the main business that you are here for is to know God, most of life's problems fall into place of their own accord.
J. I. Packer[1]

Text: 1 John 2:3-5
³ And by this we know that we have come to know him, if we keep his commandments. ⁴ Whoever says "I know him" but does not keep his commandments is a liar, and the truth is not in him, ⁵ but whoever keeps his word, in him truly the love of God is perfected. By this we may know that we are in him . . .

Thoughts:
The greatest privilege in life is the opportunity to have an intimate relationship with God. The goal of true biblical

fellowship is to know Jesus. Nothing in this world is greater than drawing closer to Christ.

John gives a great test so you can really know if you know God: if we obey His commands fully, then we are getting to know Him completely. Obedience is the true test of a growing relationship with Jesus.

Some scholars take the "knowing" described in this Scripture to mean a saving knowledge of God. But as Zane Hodges wrote:

> The idea that a Christian can believe in Christ, without knowing whether he or she has really believed, is complete nonsense.[2]

Hodges goes on to fully explain John's meaning of "knowing" Christ:

> Of course, we can know whether or not we believe. That we can know this is both common sense and completely biblical. When Jesus framed His great statement about being the Resurrection and the Life and about guaranteeing eternal life to every believer, He asked Martha, "Do you believe this?" (John 11:25–26) Martha's reply was a strong affirmation, "Yes, Lord, I believe that you are the Christ, the Son of God, who is to come into the world" (John 11:27).
>
> To the same effect is the story of the conversion of the man born blind. Jesus asks him, "Do you believe in the Son of God?" (John 9:35). When the man inquires, "Who is He, Lord, that I may believe in Him?" Jesus replies majestically, "You have both seen Him and it is He who is talking with you" (John 9:36–37). The blind man does not respond to this by saying, "I hope I believe"

or "Whether I believe or not will be seen in my works!" Such responses would have been nonsense. Instead, he says, *"Lord, I believe"* (John 9:38). The idea that a believer cannot really know he has believed is an idea without a shred of support from the Word of God.

First John 2:3 is not talking about the *saving* knowledge of Christ. It is true that all believers do indeed know God and Christ at a fundamental level; they know God as "the only true God" and they know that Jesus Christ has been sent by Him (John 17:3). But at the level of communion and fellowship, a believer may *not* know his Lord.[3]

It would be a shame to believe in Jesus and not know Him as we should. Therefore, knowing Him greater through fellowship is tested by our obedience to His commands.

Questions:

1. How is it possible to believe in God and not know Him enough to obey His commands? In what ways have you been guilty of this in your own spiritual journey?

2. John uses the same Greek word in 1 John 2:3-5 for each occurrence of the word "know." It is the New Testament word *ginosko*. This particular word means "to know especially through personal experience." It means "a first-hand acquaintance." How does the meaning of *ginosko* help with your spiritual application of 1 John 2:3-5 in your walk with God?

3. Paul, who believed strongly in Jesus, still had a great desire to know Him. Read the following words from Paul and share your thoughts on how they relate to today's Scripture.

Philippians 3:10-11 (NLT)

[10] I want to know Christ and experience the mighty power that raised Him from the dead. I want to suffer with him, sharing in his death, [11] so that one way or another I will experience the resurrection from the dead!

Day Eleven

The Letters of John

Walking Like Jesus

Only by walking with God can we hope to find the path that
leads to life. That is what it means to be a disciple.
After all, aren't we followers of Christ?
Then, by all means, let's actually follow Him.
Not ideas about Him. Not just His principles.
Let's follow Him.
John Eldredge [1]

Text: 1 John 2:6
⁶ whoever says he abides in him ought to walk in the same way
in which he walked.

Thoughts:
In this verse of Scripture, John describes the close relationship between God and believers with the phrase, "abides in
Him." John's letter picks up on the same terminology of abiding
used in Jesus' words in his Gospel:

John 15:4-7 (ESV)
⁴ "Abide in me, and I in you. As the branch cannot bear fruit
by itself, unless it abides in the vine, neither can you, unless
you abide in me. ⁵ I am the vine; you are the branches. Whoever
abides in me and I in him, he it is that bears much fruit, for apart
from me you can do nothing. ⁶ If anyone does not abide in me he

is thrown away like a branch and withers; and the branches are gathered, thrown into the fire, and burned. ⁷ If you abide in me, and my words abide in you, ask whatever you wish, and it will be done for you."

John 17:21-23 (ESV)
²¹ "that they may all be one, just as you, Father, are in me, and I in you, that they also may be in us, so that the world may believe that you have sent me. ²² The glory that you have given me I have given to them, that they may be one even as we are one, ²³ I in them and you in me, that they may become perfectly one, so that the world may know that you sent me and loved them even as you loved me."

The Greek word for "abide" is *meno*. This word means "to remain or stay, to continue to exist by persisting." When we continue steadfast in our relationship with Jesus, we can know we are living "in Him." As a branch remains connected to a tree, we are to stay attached to Jesus Christ. If the branch is severed from the tree, it will eventually die. In the same way, our abundant life is tied to our connection with our Savior and Sustainer

Abiding in Jesus leads to a life that looks like Jesus. Imitating Jesus results from a life that is intimately connected to Jesus. When a child greatly resembles one of their parents, we say, "The apple doesn't fall far from the tree." Likewise, when we are connected to the vine of Jesus Christ, the fruit doesn't fall too far from the root. The fruit of our lives will resemble the character of Christ if we abide in Him. The more we mature in our walk with Jesus, the greater our resemblance should be to our Heavenly Father.

Questions:

1. How does abiding in Christ translate into imitating Him?

2. What are your thoughts on Spurgeon's statement found below?

> Faith and obedience are bound up in the same bundle. He that obeys God, trusts God; and he that trusts God, obeys God.[2]

3. Erwin Lutzer said:

> God has a program of character development for each of us. He wants others to look at our lives and say, "He walks with God, for he lives like Christ."[3]

How is Lutzer's statement consistent with 1 John 2:6?

Day Twelve

The Letters of John

New Power for an Old Command

Whenever the strength of God is not recognized as the source
of our strength, we are breaking the First Commandment:
Do not have any gods before Me.
John Piper[1]

Text: 1 John 2:7-8
[7] Beloved, I am writing you no new commandment, but an old
commandment that you had from the beginning. The old commandment is the word that you have heard. [8] At the same time,
it is a new commandment that I am writing to you, which is
true in him and in you, because the darkness is passing away
and the true light is already shining.

Thoughts:
David Walls and Max Anders, in the *Holman New Testament
Commentary,* explain the concept found in these verses con-
cerning an old commandment that is also a new one:

> The apostle now reminds us of a new/old com-
> mandment, making a potentially confusing play on
> words. One command is at the same time both old and
> new. The command is that we should love one another.
> This command is found in the Old Testament (Leviticus
> 19:18) as well as in the Gospels (John 15:12; 13:34). In

that sense, it can be understood as an old commandment. However, the same command can also be understood as a new command in the sense that there is now new evidence and new power to fulfill it. The new evidence is that Jesus has died, been buried, and risen again. We have seen the complete example He came to show us (1 Peter 2:21), and now we have a better understanding of what love looks like than we did in Leviticus or the Gospels.

The new power is the Holy Spirit indwelling true believers, helping them to live out the commands of Scripture. In addition, the church has now gathered together to help stimulate one another to love and good deeds. Through the love Christians can show for one another, we demonstrate to the world that the light that Jesus brought into the world continues to shine in the darkness.[2]

God's commands were obeyed by Old Testament saints who simply loved God. Since they were deeply in love with the God who created them, they trusted the words God spoke to them. When God commanded Noah to build an ark, Noah obeyed even when he had never seen rain before. He loved God, so he trusted God and obeyed Him. When God commanded Abraham to leave all he knew and follow Him, Abraham left because he loved God. He had no idea where he was going, but he had a close relationship with the God he was following. When God told Joshua to march around Jericho every day for seven days, Joshua obeyed God because he had a close relationship with the One giving the orders. When the battle plan seemed strange, Joshua knew that his Commander could be trusted. All of these, and many more, Old Testament believers obeyed God's commands.

Then Jesus entered our world through a virgin birth. He lived a sinless life and died a sacrificial death. Three days after His crucifixion, Christ rose victorious over the grave. Jesus defeated sin and conquered the grave. Later, He ascended into Heaven to sit at the right hand of the throne of God. His mission was accomplished, but God still desired a relationship with His children. So, God sent the Holy Spirit to equip us, encourage us, and empower us. Now, as New Testament believers, we have His Spirit to give us the power to obey His commands. May the Holy Spirit be evident in your life as you trust in His power. May you be filled with His Spirit so that you can fully obey all of God's commands.

Questions:

1. Why is the command to love one another so important in the life of the believer?

2. What has God commanded you to do that you're still not obeying in your spiritual walk? How can you get to the point of obeying Him simply because you love Him?

3. What does John's last phrase in 1 John 2:8 have to do with your urgency to obey God's commands?

"... because the darkness is passing away and the true light is already shining."

Day Thirteen

The Letters of John

Love Shows You're Shining

We obey God's Law, not to be loved,
but because we are loved in Christ.
Jerry Bridges[1]

The fundamental principle of Christianity
is to be what God is; He is Love and He is Light.
Anonymous

Text: 1 John 2:9-11
[9] Whoever says he is in the light and hates his brother is still in darkness. [10] Whoever loves his brother abides in the light, and in him there is no cause for stumbling. [11] But whoever hates his brother is in the darkness and walks in the darkness, and does not know where he is going, because the darkness has blinded his eyes.

Thoughts:
1 John 2:8 ends this way: ". . . because the darkness is passing away and the true light is already shining." This was in reference to the new command to love one another. Believers can live progressively more in the light because the true light of Christ is already shining through them causing more of the spiritual darkness to diminish.

In light of this truth, John addressed a claim that some who professed to follow Christ were not living like true believers by noting that light and darkness cannot coincide in the same heart. Love and hate cannot either.

If you say you have the light of Jesus in you, then you cannot have hate for your brother in your heart also. In verse 11, John connects darkness to blindness. When you walk in the darkness, you cannot see the light of God's truth. Those who live in darkness are constantly stumbling because they cannot see clearly.

Theodore Epp once said, "Light reveals righteousness, and it also reveals sin."[2] Light shows the substance of what is truly there. When the light is turned on, it reveals the truth. With the spotlight of the Holy Spirit shining on your heart, your righteousness is clearly seen, and your sin is completely exposed. As G.K. Chesterton once said, "The issue is now clear. It is between light and darkness, and everyone must choose his side."

More than anything else in life, your love for others shows how brightly you are shining for Jesus. In Matthew 22:36-40, Jesus said that the greatest commandment is to love God and others. Where hate shows you are living in darkness, love proves that God's character is shining through your life.

Questions:

1. Are there any areas of your life where your profession doesn't match your practice? In other words, does what you say with your lips consistently match how you are living your life?

2. What areas do you stumble in the most in your walk with Jesus? What needs to happen to shine truth on these areas so that you can see clearly to walk in righteousness?

3. How do Jesus' words in Matthew 5:14-16 correlate with today's Scripture?

> [14] "You are the light of the world. A city set on a hill cannot be hidden. [15] Nor do people light a lamp and put it under a basket, but on a stand, and it gives light to all in the house. [16] In the same way, let your light shine before others, so that they may see your good works and give glory to your Father who is in heaven."

Day Fourteen

The Letters of John

The Benefits in His Family

You are a child of God. He is Father of your spirit. Spiritually you are of noble birth, the offspring of the King of Heaven. Fix that truth in your mind and hold on to it. However many generations in your mortal ancestry, no matter what race or people you represent, the pedigree of your spirit can be written on a single line. You are a child of God!
Boyd K. Packer[1]

Text: 1 John 2:12-14
[12] I am writing to you, little children,
  because your sins are forgiven for his name's sake.
[13] I am writing to you, fathers,
  because you know him who is from the beginning.
I am writing to you, young men,
  because you have overcome the evil one.
I write to you, children,
  because you know the Father.
[14] I write to you, fathers,
  because you know him who is from the beginning.
I write to you, young men,
  because you are strong,
  and the word of God abides in you,
  and you have overcome the evil one.

Thoughts:

There has been much debate around these verses concerning the meaning of "fathers, young men, and children." Some scholars believe that these terms speak to three different groups of people according to their physical ages. Other people say that these are three levels of spiritual maturity in the life of a believer. We do know that John is writing to believers about their fellowship with God.

Let's look first at what John says that little children know. Little children in God's family know that their sins are forgiven. God forgives your sins the moment you are born again into His family through salvation. The greatest and first blessing for any believer is that God has taken away their sins.

Scripture teaches that God does four things when He forgives your sin at the point of salvation. Psalm 103:12 points out that God removes our sin "as far as the East is from the West." Jeremiah 31:34 declares that when God forgives, He "remembers our sins no more." Isaiah 38:17 states that God has "cast all my sins behind His back." Micah 7:19 announces that God "cast all our sins into the depths of the sea." All these pictures show what God does to the sins of His "little children." The moment we are born again spiritually, the greatest benefit of all has taken place.

John says that children "know the Father" (1 John 2:13). But the older you grow spiritually, the more you should know your Father. Next, John states what fathers know. Fathers know "him who is from the beginning." Twice, in these verses, John said that he wrote these things so that fathers will know the God who has no beginning. As we grow and mature in Christ, we understand that we know the God of eternity. He is the God who always was, and who will forever be. When we grow into spiritual maturity, we begin to understand that God is bigger than we can fathom. As God told Isaiah:

Isaiah 55:8-9 (ESV)

[8] For my thoughts are not your thoughts, neither are your ways my ways, declares the Lord. [9] For as the heavens are higher than the earth, so are my ways higher than your ways and my thoughts than your thoughts.

"Little children" know they are forgiven and that they know the Father. "Fathers" begin to grasp the enormity of God. In between, "young men overcome the evil one." Spiritual growing young men are "strong and the word of God abides in" them. That is how they overcome the evil one. The Word of God gives them strength to battle the evil one.

John writes his letters so that believers will realize what they should know as they grow up in Christ. If you know what you should know in your growing relationship with Jesus, you realize that God has blessed you with tremendous benefits that come from being in His family.

Questions:

1. Where are you currently in the growth pattern of your Christian life? What has caused spiritual growth spurts? What has stunted your spiritual growth?

2. What you know in your relationship with God shows how much you have grown. Are you continually learning more about God as you grow up spiritually? What is God currently teaching you about Himself?

3. Spend some time today reflecting on the following quote from Max Lucado.

> "To call yourself a child of God is one thing. To be called a child of God by those who watch your life is another thing altogether."[2]

Day Fifteen

The Letters of John

Strong Words About Love

Loving the world begins in the heart
before it is ever lived out in our lives.
David L. Allen[1]

Text: 1 John 2:15-16

[15] Do not love the world or the things in the world. If anyone loves the world, the love of the Father is not in him. [16] For all that is in the world—the desires of the flesh and the desires of the eyes and pride of life—is not from the Father but is from the world.

Thoughts:

The beloved disciple John enters into a convincing argument concerning love in 1 John 2:15-16. Before we can understand the full application of this Scripture, we need to dig deeper into the original meaning of his words:

There are two keywords in this passage: "love" and "world." Both of these words must be unpacked as to their meaning to understand John's point. "World" (*kosmos*) is used in three primary ways in the New Testament. It is sometimes used to refer to Planet Earth. We sometimes talk about "the world" when we mean the earth. That is not the meaning here. It is often used to refer to people, as in John 3:16: "For God so loved the world." That is not the meaning here either. Sometimes the word "world" is used to refer to the organized evil system with its principles and practices, all under the authority of Satan, which includes all teachings, ideas, culture, attitudes, activities, etc., that are opposed to God. A fixation on the material over the spiritual, promotion of self over others, pleasure over principle – these are just a few descriptors of the world system John is talking about. The word "world" here means everything that opposes Christ and his work on earth. Jesus called Satan "the ruler of this world" (John 14:30; 16:11), and Paul called him "the god of this world" (2 Corinthians 4:4). In Luke 16:8, Jesus referred to all unsaved people as "the sons of this world."

Let's also unpack the word "love." We use the word *love* in so many different contexts in the English language. We love pizza. We love football. We love our job. We love our spouse. We love fishing, hunting, food, art, etc. With all this variety, what exactly does *love* mean? In its essence, love is two things: a desire for something and a commitment to something.

The word John used is the verb form of *agapē*, and it is a word that the Christians took from common Greek vocabulary and invested with new meaning.

John hits his readers right between the eyes in verse 15 with a knockout punch. Significantly, the exhortation to stop loving the world is the first overt imperative in the letter. John assumes that, to some extent, some of his readers were guilty of loving the world system. John also exhorts Christians not to love "the things in the world." Some Christians had become too cozy with the world system. They had begun to compromise with the world. They were giving too much ground to the world's way of thinking and acting. Things in the world began to look more and more glamorous. Some Christians had taken their eyes off Jesus and put them on the things of the world. [2]

In these verses, John makes it clear that it is impossible to love God and the world at the same time. Then he gives three major descriptions of the world: the desires of the flesh, the desires of the eyes, and the pride of life. "The desires of the flesh" include all the desires that come from our sinful nature. Someone who is in love with the world lives a life dominated by their sinful senses. "The desires of the eyes" means we crave what we see. The eyes are the gateway to our thoughts. If our eyes are on Jesus, our thoughts are on Him also. However, if our eyes are on the things of this world, then our focus is shifted to worldly things. "The pride of life" describes the arrogant nature of those who live their lives focused on themselves. This last phrase portrays a person who is more in love with themselves than with Jesus.

John used convicting language to teach us that those who love Jesus Christ live in opposition to the world. He also made it clear that to love the world places you in conflict with God. Either you are in love with Jesus, or you are in love with the world. The simple but strong truth is you cannot love them both.

Questions:

1. After reading today's Scripture and devotion, honestly answer the following question and explain your answer:

Who do you currently love: the world or Jesus?

2. Describe in what ways you are tempted to love the world based on John's three following descriptions:

"The desires of the flesh"

"The desires of the eyes"

"pride of life"

3. What are your thoughts on the following quote that began today's devotion?

"Loving the world begins in the heart before it is ever lived out in our lives."

Day Sixteen

The Letters of John

Abiding Forever

Once a person is united with God,
how could he not live forever?
C.S. Lewis

At most, you will live a hundred years on earth,
but you will spend forever in eternity.
Rick Warren[1]

Text: 1 John 2:17
[17] And the world is passing away along with its desires, but whoever does the will of God abides forever.

Thoughts:
The word "forever" is hard to comprehend. We live in a world defined by time frames. We hit snooze on our alarm clock, and we can sleep exactly five more minutes. A normal workday is exactly eight hours. A pregnancy normally lasts nine months. We go to school for twelve years. We are confined by time in a world that has deadlines. Our world is fast paced because we have time constraints. If you don't believe me, just count how many times you check your watch before the day is over.

After John said, "Do not love the world" (1 John 2:15), he said, "the world is passing away along with its desires" (1 John

2:17). If you are in love with the world, that relationship will not last. If your desires are not for God, they are temporary cravings. Why not put your passion into a relationship that never ends? Why waste your time with momentary desires when you can pursue a relationship that endures forever?

Notice just a few Scriptures that focus on "forever":

Isaiah 40:8 (ESV)

The grass withers, the flower fades, but the word of our God will stand forever.

Lamentations 5:19 (ESV)

But you, O Lord, reign forever; your throne endures to all generations.

Psalm 73:26 (ESV)

My flesh and my heart may fail, but God is the strength of my heart and my portion forever.

John 14:16 (ESV)

"And I will ask the Father, and he will give you another Helper, to be with you forever,"

Psalm 23:6 (ESV)

Surely goodness and mercy shall follow me all the days of my life, and I shall dwell in the house of the Lord forever.

Psalm 16:11 (ESV)

You make known to me the path of life; in your presence there is fullness of joy; at your right hand are pleasures forevermore.

Scripture records the word "forever" 478 times and the phrase "eternal life" 41 times. God wants you to know that life with Him lasts forever.

John Wesley once said, "I judge all things only by the price they shall gain in eternity."[2] This is an incredible principle that should be the perspective by which we evaluate our lives.

F.B. Meyer wrote, "God has set eternity in our heart, and man's infinite capacity cannot be filled or satisfied with the things of time and this world." [3] At this point, a simple reminder of John's words in 1 John 2:17 is all that is needed: "And the world is passing away along with its desires, but whoever does the will of God abides forever."

Questions:

1. In what specific ways can you love and live in light of eternity?

2. Consider the following quote by C.S. Lewis in light of 1 John 2:17.

> Christianity asserts that every individual human being is going to live forever, and this must be either true or false. Now there are a good many things that would not be worth bothering about if I were going to live only seventy years, but which I had better bother about very seriously if I am going to live forever.[4]

3. What does the following famous Scripture teach about your eternal relationship with Jesus Christ?

John 3:16 (ESV)

"For God so loved the world, that he gave his only Son, that whoever believes in him should not perish but have eternal life."

Day Seventeen

The Essential Truth

Every spirit that does not confess Jesus is not from God.
This is the spirit of the antichrist, which you heard was coming
and now is in the world already.
1 John 4:3

Text: 1 John 2:18
[18] Children, it is the last hour, and as you have heard that anti-christ is coming, so now many antichrists have come.
Therefore we know that it is the last hour.

Thoughts:
We live in a world that has coined the phrase "The truth hurts." This phrase typically means that hearing or facing the truth can be emotionally painful or especially difficult if it contradicts someone's beliefs or expectations. While the truth sometimes hurts, the essential truth always helps. While accepting the truth at times can be challenging, it is ultimately necessary for proper spiritual growth.

Arizona Pastor Stephen J. Cole made the following comments in a sermon on 1 John 2:18:

We live in a day when the whole idea of spiritual discernment is minimized because spiritual truth is minimized. The slogan is, "Doctrine divides. Let's set aside our doctrinal differences and come together on the areas where we agree." Another popular mantra is, "Jesus said that they will know that we are His disciples by our *love*, *not* by our *doctrine*." The implication is, "Set aside your doctrinal views and accept anyone who says that he believes in Jesus." Tolerance, unity, and love are viewed as much more important than doctrinal truth, which often smacks of pride.

I have had my share of unpleasant encounters with those who arrogantly claim to have the truth. They beat you up with it, not showing much grace or kindness. But we should not allow such experiences to cause us to throw out the biblical emphasis on sound doctrine. It is *not* a minor theme in the Bible!

It is highly significant that John, the apostle of love, who has just written that love is an essential mark of the true Christian (2:7–11), now calls these false teachers "antichrists" and "liars"! He doesn't call them "brothers in Christ," who just have different ways of understanding things. He makes it plain that they were trying to deceive the true Christians and that they were not Christian in any sense of the term. True biblical love is not divorced from an emphasis on biblical truth. To compromise the truth about the person and work of Jesus Christ is to be hateful to the core because such error results in the eternal damnation of those who embrace it.[1]

If we are to become all that God has planned for His children, we must accept the truth of His Word. In Ephesians 4:15-16, we find these words:

[15] Rather, speaking the truth in love, we are to grow up in every way into him who is the head, into Christ, [16] from

whom the whole body, joined and held together by every joint with which it is equipped, when each part is working properly, makes the body grow so that it builds itself up in love.

The truth that John brings to the forefront in 1 John 2:18 is these believers were living in the last days in a world that contains the spirit of the antichrist. John Wesley said:

> With the term antichrist, or the spirit of antichrist, he includes all false teachers, and enemies of the truth; yea whatever doctrines or men are contrary to Christ.[2]

Wesley goes on to say that even though the apostle Paul mentions "the man of sin" (2 Thessalonians 2:3), John's use of the term "antichrist" tends to refer to being anti-Christian rather than one specific person.[3]

Therefore, John is writing to a group of Christ-followers being challenged by those who were in opposition to Christ. These anti-Christians were teaching concepts that sought to disprove what Christ did, in an attempt to deny who Christ was. John encouraged the believers to resist such lies by remaining true to their relationship with Jesus in the last days.

Questions:

1. How do you remain faithful to the truth of who God is while living in a world full of people who live in opposition to Christ? In what ways do you see yourself living in the last days?

2. Wesleyan scholars David Case and David Holdren give the following statements in their commentary on 1 John 2:18:

> It is William Barclay who reminds us that in a very real sense, every hour is the last hour for somebody, someplace. This is true not only in terms of death, but also in terms of facing choices that involve aiding the cause of Christ, giving this concept an ever-current relevance.[4]

What are your thoughts on these statements in reference to John's words "Children, it is the last hour. . ."?

3. Read John's words concerning Jesus in his Gospel.

John 1:14 (ESV)
And the Word became flesh and dwelt among us, and we have seen his glory, glory as of the only Son from the Father, full of grace and truth.

How does John's description of Jesus as "grace" and "truth" depict how His followers are to live in a world full of darkness?

Day Eighteen

The Letters of John

Not of Us

Not everyone who is with us is of us.
Anonymous

Text: 1 John 2:19

¹⁹ They went out from us, but they were not of us; for if they had been of us, they would have continued with us. But they went out, that it might become plain that they all are not of us.

Thoughts:

Remember that John had previously warned his fellow believers that they were living in the last hour among the spirit of the antichrist. Now, John tells them that these false teachers had come from their own group. Imagine how surprised these believers were to hear that these people "went out from us, but they were not of us."

So, just in 1 John 2:18-19, we have read about the following: "last hour," "antichrist," and "they went out from us." These words from John have been difficult for many interpreters down through the ages. Let's get Charles Swindoll's insights to guide us through today's Scripture:

False teachers usually come from within the church (2:19). John says these antichrists "went out from us," indicating a departure from the true, apostolic churches.

Throughout history – and even today – many cult founders formerly belonged to strong, Bible-believing churches. But they rebelled against their orthodox upbringing, failing to be either discipled or disciplined. They broke away to teach different doctrines and embrace contrary lifestyles.

In addition, false teachers never truly experienced the saving grace of Jesus Christ (1 John 2:19). The fact that these false teachers so drastically departed from the core teachings of the true faith demonstrates that they were "not really of us." Had those antichrists been true fellow members of the body of Christ (not just physically but also spiritually) and had they been truly united to Him by the regenerating work of the Holy Spirit, they "would have remained" with the true church. Their departure makes it clear that "they all are not of us."[2]

May author David Jackman's words give us the proper biblical application of today's Scripture:

We need to make sure that we continue in the fellowship of like-minded Christians. We need one another, not to boost our flagging morale, but to encourage one another in the things that matter most. If we belong to Christ, then we belong to his people and the mark of belonging is remaining. When the going gets tough, when the grass looks greener on the other side, when our fellow Christians seem not to understand us, when the latest novelty in teaching or experience looks exciting and liberating, then we need God's people. With all our imperfections and idiosyncrasies, we belong to one another because we belong to him. And ultimately, we prove the reality of our love by our loyalty.

It is a dangerous hour. There are plenty of hostile forces at work. What we believe does matter, as does our fellowship with other Christians. We need to be realistic about our enemy, but confident in our Savior. Let the apostle Peter have the last word on the same theme: "Be self-controlled and alert. Your enemy the devil prowls around like a roaring lion looking for someone to devour. Resist him, standing firm in the faith, because you know that your brothers throughout the world are undergoing the same kind of suffering." (1 Peter 5:8–9).[3]

Questions:

1. In light of today's devotion, why is it essential that you know the truth of God's Word? Why is it critical that you continue to grow closer to Christ?

2. How can you live sold-out for Jesus in the fellowship of His people, while at the same time, guarding your heart against deception?

3. How are Paul's words to Timothy a wise warning for all believers as we live in the "last hour"?

2 Timothy 4:3-4 (ESV)
   [3] For the time is coming when people will not endure sound teaching, but having itching ears they will accumulate for themselves teachers to suit their own passions, [4] and will turn away from listening to the truth and wander off into myths.

Day Nineteen

The Letters of John

Anointed To Know the Truth

We have an unction from the Lord to live our lives for Him.
What is an **unction**? It is derived from the word *chrisma*, which
means "anointing." Bible scholars believe this is a reference to
the anointing of the Holy Spirit
who indwells the Christian the moment he or she
puts faith in Jesus Christ for salvation.
Rod Mattoon [1]

Text: 1 John 2:20-23

[20] But you have been anointed by the Holy One, and you all
have knowledge. [21] I write to you, not because you do not know
the truth, but because you know it, and because no lie is of
the truth. [22] Who is the liar but he who denies that Jesus is the
Christ? This is the antichrist, he who denies the Father and the
Son. [23] No one who denies the Son has the Father. Whoever confesses the Son has the Father also.

Thoughts:

The Life Application Bible Commentary provides a great introduction to today's topic of anointing:

> John wrote of Christians being anointed. It has
> become commonplace to label certain preachers,
> songs, worship services, or sermons as "anointed."

That usually means the person somehow evokes or facilitates an awareness of God's power or presence. But this wonderful quality is not what the word "anointed" means. To "anoint" in biblical terminology simply means to consecrate or set apart for a special purpose. Kings and priests were anointed with oil in solemn ceremonies intended to designate them as civil and spiritual leaders. But now the Spirit of God anoints every believer upon conversion (1 Corinthians 12:13). Because we Christians have received this anointing, we can be assured of the basis for our salvation and the Spirit-filled life.[2]

We live in a world full of false teachers who seek to distort the truth and deceive followers of Jesus Christ. But God has given us the anointing from the Holy Spirit so that we will know the truth. The same John who wrote 1 John recorded these words from Jesus in John 16:13:

> [13] "When the Spirit of truth comes, he will guide you into all the truth, for he will not speak on his own authority, but whatever he hears he will speak, and he will declare to you the things that are to come."

The Holy Spirit guides the believer in all truth. He can't help but speak the truth because He is the Spirit of truth. When a person is saved, the Holy Spirit comes to indwell the new believer with the truths of God. The Holy Spirit filling a believer's heart is God's defense against the lies of the enemy.

John goes on to call out the specific lie of those in opposition to Christ. A liar denies that Jesus is the Savior of the world. Anyone who denies the Son does not know the Father. Therefore, you can always tell when someone is a false teacher because they will deny that Jesus Christ is God's Son.

A person who has been anointed by the Holy Spirit will confess that Jesus Christ is the Son of the Father. Notice the Spirit's own confession of Christ at His baptism as recorded in Luke 3:21-22:

> **21** Now when all the people were baptized, and when Jesus also had been baptized and was praying, the heavens were opened, **22** and the Holy Spirit descended on him in bodily form, like a dove; and a voice came from heaven, "You are my beloved Son; with you I am well pleased."

The Spirit of truth must confess that Jesus is the Christ. Those who are anointed with the Spirit of truth must do the same.

Questions:

1. In what ways are you encouraged today by the fact that "the Spirit of truth will guide you into all truth"? (John 16:13)

2. William Tyndale once made the following statement about the anointing of the Holy Spirit:

> You are not anointed with oil in your bodies, but with the Spirit of Christ in your souls. The Spirit teaches you all truth in Christ, and makes you able to judge what is a lie, and what is truth, and to know Christ from the antichrist.[3]

What are your thoughts about Tyndale's statement in light of today's Scripture?

3. How does God's promise of the Holy Spirit in John 14:16-17 to His first disciples give you confidence as you live as His disciple in a world full of deception?

> **16** "And I will ask the Father, and he will give you another Helper, to be with you forever, **17** even the Spirit of truth, whom the world cannot receive, because it neither sees him nor knows him. You know him, for he dwells with you and will be in you."

4. List the characteristics of the Holy Spirit found in John 14:16-17 that assure you that you are anointed to know the truth.

Day Twenty

The Letters of John

Let What You Heard Abide

To have His words abiding in us, is to keep His sayings and
precepts continually before our memories and minds, and to
make them the guide of our actions and the rule of our daily
conduct and behavior.

J.C. Ryle[1]

Text: 1 John 2:24-25

²⁴ Let what you heard from the beginning abide in you. If what
you heard from the beginning abides in you, then you too will
abide in the Son and in the Father. ²⁵ And this is the promise that
he made to us – eternal life.

Thoughts:

Remember that John wrote the Gospel of John, the Letters
of John, and the Book of Revelation. In Revelation, John wrote
the following phrase seven times:

He who has an ear, let him hear what the Spirit says to
the churches. (See Revelation 2:7,11,17,29; 3:6,13,22.)

Why did John close the message to each of the seven churches with the exact same phrase? I believe it is a verbal warning to
pay careful attention to what has just been said.

Jesus implored the use of this same message in the following Scriptures: Matthew 11:15, 13:9, 13:43; Mark 4:23; and Luke 8:8. Jesus wanted to make sure that people didn't let His words go in one ear and out the other.

In 1 John 2:24, John writes, "Let what you heard from the beginning abide in you." As far as listening is concerned, we can all grow to become better listeners.

Writer Charles Swindoll told the story about a time in his life when God taught him a lesson about listening:

> I once found myself with too many commitments in too few days. I got extremely nervous and tense about it. I was snapping at my wife and our children, choking down my food at mealtimes, and feeling irritated at those unexpected interruptions throughout the day. Before long, things around our home started reflecting the pattern of my hurry-up lifestyle. It was becoming unbearable.
>
> I distinctly remember after supper one evening, the words of our younger daughter, Colleen. She wanted to tell me something important that had happened to her at school that day. She began hurriedly, "Daddy, I want to tell you something and I'll tell you really fast."
>
> Suddenly realizing her frustration, I answered, "Honey, you can tell me – and you don't have to tell me really fast. Say it slowly." I'll never forget her answer. She said, "Then listen slowly."

Maybe, if we listened to God slowly, we would learn to abide in Him. Remember, the word "abide" means "to remain." Even the definition of the word abide implies slowing down and spending some time lingering.

Questions:

1. When God speaks, how can you learn to be a better listener? In what specific ways can you mature in letting God's Word abide in you?

2. Warren Wiersbe wrote the following statement in his book entitled *Abide*:

> *"It is the Holy Spirit who encourages and enables us to abide. He teaches us the Word; He enables us to pray; He reveals our sins; He gives us the inward desire to obey God."*[4]

Contemplate Wiersbe's statement today and "let what you heard abide in you."

3. How does God's promise of eternal life keep you strong as you abide in Him? What does God's commitment to you mean as you seek to draw closer to Him?

Day Twenty-One

The Letters of John

Taught To Abide in Him

Abiding is a journey of growing spiritual roots down deep so
that you can do more than just survive, you can thrive.
Anonymous

Text: 1 John 2:26-27
[26] I write these things to you about those who are trying to
deceive you. [27] But the anointing that you received from him
abides in you, and you have no need that anyone should
teach you. But as his anointing teaches you about everything, and is true, and is no lie – just as it has taught you,
abide in him.

Thoughts:
    The Holy Spirit teaches us truths about God. These truths
strengthen our faith and give us greater confidence to abide
in Christ. John writes, ". . . His anointing teaches you about
everything that is true . . ." One of the Holy Spirit's main roles
is Teacher, and His major characteristic is truth.

John 14:26 (ESV)
    [26] "But the Helper, the Holy Spirit, whom the Father will send
in my name, he will teach you all things and bring to your re-
membrance all that I have said to you."

John 15:26 (ESV)

[26] "But when the Helper comes, whom I will send to you from the Father, the Spirit of truth, who proceeds from the Father, he will bear witness about me."

John 16:23 (ESV)

[23] "In that day you will ask nothing of me. Truly, truly, I say to you, whatever you ask of the Father in my name, he will give it to you."

1 John 5:6b (ESV)

[6b] And the Spirit is the one who testifies, because the Spirit is the truth.

The Holy Spirit will always speak the truth because that is who He is. In addition, His truths will always instruct and guide. He cannot help but teach, because His purpose is to train.

John continues in verse 27 by stating, ". . . just as it has taught you, abide in Him." The "it" in this statement is the "anointing." The Holy Spirit has touched your life and set you apart for the purpose of abiding in Jesus Christ. The greatest lesson the Holy Spirit ever teaches is the truth found in abiding daily in a growing relationship with Jesus Christ.

Men and women of faith have found their sole strength to thrive spiritually through abiding in Jesus Christ. Notice how the following statements from two great missionaries center on abiding in Christ:

Amy Carmichael – Missionary to India

"So again and yet again we ask you to pray for the movement of the breath of God, and far more for us His workers here, that we may abide in Him without Whom we can do nothing."[1]

Hudson Taylor – Missionary to China

After a period of spiritual struggle, while serving and leading in China, Hudson Taylor discovered the truth of abiding in Christ from John 15. In a letter to his sister, Taylor described his experience with this truth from God's Word:

"As I thought of the Vine and the branches, what light the blessed Spirit poured directly into my soul! How great seemed my mistake in having wished to get the sap, the fulness out of Him. I saw not only that Jesus would never leave me, but that I was a member of His body, of His flesh, and of His bones. The vine now I see, is not the root merely, but all – root, stem, branches, twigs, leaves, flowers, fruit: and Jesus is not only that: He is soil and sunshine, air and showers, and ten thousand times more than we have ever dreamed, wished for, or needed. Oh, the joy of seeing this truth! I do pray that the eyes of your understanding may be enlightened, that you may know and enjoy the riches freely given us in Christ."[2]

Questions:

1. How do the truths from great men and women of faith strengthen your faith to abide?

2. Imagine if you left everyone you knew and traveled to a foreign country to serve as a missionary. How would your total dependence on Jesus encourage you daily and provide hope to sustain you? Since this world is not our home, how can we all learn to abide more in Jesus and spiritually live on mission with Him?

3. How does Psalm 91:1-2 provide you with even more faith to abide?

> ¹He who dwells in the shelter of the Most High will abide in the shadow of the Almighty. ²I will say to the Lord, "My refuge and my fortress, my God, in whom I trust."

Day Twenty-Two

The Letters of John

When He Appears

Let us be alert to the season in which we are living. It is the season of the Blessed Hope, calling for us to cut our ties with the world and build ourselves on this One who will soon appear. He is our hope—a Blessed Hope enabling us to rise above our times and fix our gaze upon Him.
A.W. Tozer[1]

Text: 1 John 2:28
[28] And now, little children, abide in him, so that when he appears we may have confidence and not shrink from him in shame at his coming.

Thoughts:

John Wesley was once asked how he would react if he knew that Christ was coming that very night. His instant reply was, "I don't think I would change any of my plans."[2] That is a great response from a man who was daily living in readiness for the return of Christ.

John used a very interesting word for "confidence" in the original language of 1 John 2:28. It is the Greek word *parrhesia*. This is a compound New Testament word that comes from two words: the word *pas*, which means "all," and the word *rhesis*, which is "as statement quoted with resolve." Together, the word *parrhesia* means "a bold statement made with resolve."

When you are abiding in Christ, your life will make a bold statement about your true faith in Jesus. When you live your life fully committed to Him, one day you will be able to stand before Him with confidence. You will know that He knows how much you truly love Him.

Notice how the following Scriptures describe the confidence we can have when we know Christ intimately:

Hebrews 4:16 (ESV)

[16] Let us then with confidence draw near to the throne of grace, that we may receive mercy and find grace to help in time of need.

Hebrews 10:35-36 (ESV)

[35] Therefore do not throw away your confidence, which has a great reward. [36] For you have need of endurance, so that when you have done the will of God you may receive what is promised.

Ephesians 3:11-12 (ESV)

[11] This was according to the eternal purpose that he has realized in Christ Jesus our Lord, [12] in whom we have boldness and access with confidence through our faith in him.

There is a huge contrast between the word "shame" and the term "confidence." They are the exact opposite of one another. The phrase "and not shrink from Him in shame" comes from a Greek word that means "to dishonor or disgrace." When you disgrace someone by the way you live your life, and then you see them, your shame causes you to withdraw from them. You know you have completely dishonored that person, so you are overcome with shame and guilt in their presence.

When Christ appears, you will either stand before Him in confidence, or you will shrink back in shame. The determining factor will be whether or not you are abiding in Him.

Questions:

1. If Jesus came back at this very moment, would you have confidence or shame? Explain the reason for your answer.

2. Spend some time today envisioning the return of Christ. What do you think that moment will be like? May the following Scripture help to get you started:

Revelation 1:7 (ESV)
⁷ Behold, he is coming with the clouds, and every eye will see him, even those who pierced him, and all tribes of the earth will wail on account of him. Even so. Amen.

3. What other Scripture comes to mind that could help you with your vision of His Second Coming?

Day Twenty-Three

The Letters of John

If You Know You Know

To be born again is, as it were, to enter upon a new existence, to have a new mind, a new heart, new views, new principles, new tastes, new affections, new likes, new dislikes, new fears, new joys, new sorrows, new love to things once hated, and new hatred to things once loved.
J.C. Ryle [1]

Text: 1 John 2:29
[29] If you know that he is righteous, you may be sure that everyone who practices righteousness has been born of him.

Thoughts:
We live in a day and age where most people use abbreviations on texts and social media. If you are like me, you have to ask your kids what they mean because you have no idea. For over a year I thought that LOL meant "lots of love." Imagine my embarrassment when I finally discovered that those letters are short for "laughing out loud." I did laugh out loud when I finally understood what it meant!

One that took me a long time to figure out was IYKYK, which stands for "If you know, you know." This sentiment is the one the apostle John must have had in mind when he wrote 1 John 1:29.

In the English translation, you might miss John's "If you know, you know." The English Standard Version translates this first part of this verse as, "If you know that He is righteous, you may be sure that . . ." However, John uses two different Greek words for "knowledge" in this verse: "If you know (*eidete*), you know (*ginoskete*). The first "know" is an absolute and intuitive type of knowledge. The word means "to be aware of the facts." The second "know," translated "be sure of," is a word that means, "knowledge learned or gained by experience."

John combined these two words for "knowledge" to describe how a person can know they are born again spiritually. If you have the absolute knowledge of the fact that God is righteous, then you can know by experience that those who practice righteousness are born of God. One sure way to know that you are saved is because true righteousness can only be practiced by those who possess the righteous nature of their Father through a spiritual birth.

The word for righteous in this verse is *dikaios*. *Dikaios* is derived from the word that means, "right, judicial approval by God." This word is used in Scripture to describe what is right and just according to God's standard.

John is in no way saying that good moral behavior is a sure way to know that you are saved. His word choice specifically points to correct behavior acceptable to God that can only occur in the heart of a sinful person through a supernatural spiritual birth. When you live a supernatural life that leads to righteousness approved by God, you know that God's power is living through you. When your life is characterized by the righteousness of God, you can be sure that you have been born again. IYKYK! If you know, you know!

Questions:

1. How does Jesus's discussion with Nicodemus in John 3 relate to what John writes here in 1 John 2:29?

2. Read the following quote by J.I. Packer:

> "The gift of sonship to God becomes ours not through being born, but through being born again."[2]

How can Packer's statement help you to know that you have been born of God?

3. How can you distinguish between good works done in human strength and the righteousness that only comes from God?

4. R.C. Sproul once said:

"The only works of righteousness that serve to justify a sinner are the works of Christ."[3]

How does this statement coincide with today's devotion?

Day Twenty-Four

The Letters of John

The Love of The Father

The love of God is like the Amazon River
flowing down to water one daisy.
Anonymous[1]

Text: 1 John 3:1

[1] See what kind of love the Father has given to us, that we should be called children of God; and so we are. The reason why the world does not know us is that it did not know him.

Thoughts:

We will discover this truth in the last half of 1 John 4:8: "God is love." Considering this truth, Dr. David Jeremiah told the following story in his book, *God Loves You: He Always Has--He Always Will*:

In the days when the great evangelist Dwight L. Moody was preaching in Chicago, a poor drunkard stumbled up the steps to the front door of Moody's church. The man pushed the door open, scanned the room, and saw no one inside. His eyes, however, were drawn to a large sign hanging above the pulpit that read "God Is Love." It struck him with anger. He slammed the door, and staggered down the steps, muttering, "God is not love. If God was love He would love me, and He doesn't love a miserable man like me. It isn't true."

He went on his way, but those words were burning inside him, *God is love. God is love. God is love.* He couldn't resist, *Was it true? Is it possible?* After a while, he turned around, retraced his steps, and entered the church again, confused and desperate. By now, the people had gathered, and as Moody began to preach, the man slipped into a seat in the back corner. He wept during the entire sermon as anger and confusion began to give way to joy and hope.

Afterward, Moody made his way to the door to shake hands with the people as they left. But the man didn't leave. He remained in his seat, weeping. Moody came over, sat down beside him, and asked, "What are you crying about, my friend? What was it in the sermon that touched your heart?"

"Oh, Mr. Moody, I didn't hear a word that you spoke tonight," the man responded. "It's those words up there over your pulpit, 'God Is Love,' that broke my heart." Moody sat down and explained to him the depths of God's love. The man listened and gave his heart to God, understanding for the first time that God really did love him.[2]

If we could just see what kind of love God has given to us, it would change everything. The word John uses for "see" in 1 John 3:1 is the Greek word *horao*. This word means, "to perceive or discern" and "to properly see." It can mean metaphorically to see with your mind, and spiritually "to discern inwardly." Some translators interpret this word as "behold."

God wants you to know how much He loves you. Your Heavenly Father desires for you to know with your mind and your heart that He is love. Love is the essence of who God is. Since God is love, He must love you. He can't help Himself. Everything God has done for you is because He loves you. God sent His Son because He "so loved the world" (John 3:16). Romans 5:8 tells us that, "God demonstrated His own love for us in this: while we were still sinners, Christ died for us."

Oswald Chambers reaffirmed that God is love when he wrote, "The love of God is not created – it is His nature."[4] Therefore, as you grow closer to God, you will realize more about His love. When you behold Him, you can't help but see that He loves you.

Questions:

1. What kind of love has the Father given to you?

2. What does it mean for you to be called a child of God?

3. How important are John's words, ". . . and so we are"? Why?

4. As you consider today how much God loves you, reflect on this statement by Charles Spurgeon:

"Nothing binds me to my Lord like a strong belief in His changeless love."[5]

Day Twenty-Five

The Letters of John

Currently Great with a Greater Future

The most thrilling thing about Heaven is that Jesus Christ will
be there. I will see Him face to face. Jesus Christ will meet us
at the end of our journey.
Billy Graham[1]

Text: 1 John 3:2
² Beloved, we are God's children now, and what we will be has
not yet appeared; but we know that when he appears we shall
be like him, because we shall see him as he is.

Thoughts:
John begins today's verse with a statement of where we are
right now spiritually. We are God's children right now if we have
been born again. No one has to wait until Heaven to become
His son or daughter. Every believer is a child of God at this very
moment. John emphasizes the fact before he even talks about
the future.

So currently we are not poor little victims of our culture just
barely surviving down here on Earth until we can get to Heaven
in the sweet by and by. We are not sinners who every once and
a while can do a saintly thing. We are blood-bought children of
the God who is both Creator and King! In our Father's eyes, we
are saints who still have the potential to sin. We are more than
overcomers because God loves us. (See Romans 8:37.) God lav-

ished His love on us so that we could carry the title of His children. (See 1 John 3:1.)

When you think it can't get any better than being called God's child, John moves on to our future with God. As God's child now, we are great. But our future is even greater than our present. One day, "we shall be like Him" and "we will see Him as He is."

The authors of the *Life Application Bible Commentary* give the following explanation of 1 John 3:2:

> Something inconceivably wonderful is waiting for God's children, even more glorious than what they now possess. Christians have been born into God's family, and they presently enjoy God's kindness and blessings through Christ. But in the future, they will also fully share in His glory. Believers have a vision of it now, but it will be reality when their bodies are resurrected. Believers don't yet know the specifics because these haven't been revealed, but they do *know that when He is revealed, they shall be like Him.* This hints at what this future glory will be like, though the world is completely ignorant of it: Christ will be revealed to His people and in his people in all his glory, as the very likeness of God (2 Corinthians 4:4)—and His people will be like Him! In the same way, believers will be revealed to the world as God's children, sharing in Christ's glory and beauty.[2]

Questions:

1. How can you live the abundant life now that your Father desires for you? What does His great love have to do with the greatness of your present life?

2. How can you live a greater life spiritually knowing what awaits you in Heaven?

3. Do you think you will be surprised on that day when you see Him as He is? What preconceived cultural ideas about God do you think will be exposed when you see who He really is?

Day Twenty-Six

The Letters of John

Hope Purifies

Biblical hope is life-changing certainty about the future.
Biblical hope is being certain about the future
in a way that affects how you live now.
Tim Keller[1]

Text: 1 John 3:3
[3] And everyone who thus hopes in him purifies himself as he
is pure.

Thoughts:

In *A Commentary for Bible Students*, we find these great
words of application under a discussion of 1 John 3:3:

> There is the wonderful biblical teaching of Christ's
> return to earth, called the Second Advent. For centuries,
> and particularly in the first century, believers thought
> Christ would return in their lifetime. Of course, God's
> timing is not always what we want or expect. The con-
> servative, evangelical churches of the twentieth century
> taught that Jesus was coming soon. Some even dared
> to predict when He would return. They were, of course,
> wrong.
>
> We need to quit predicting and start proclaiming the
> motto "Live ready." That way, whenever Christ returns,

we will share the glory! That's our second coming theology: First, He *will* return. Second, live *ready*.[2]

As believers in Jesus Christ, we have the certain hope that Jesus will one day return, and we will be joined together with Him in glory. One day we will all stand before our God and our lives will be evaluated and rewarded accordingly. If we live daily considering this future moment, we will be motivated to pursue holiness.

After Jesus returns, everyone will stand before the Lord. Paul hints at this encounter in Philippians 2:9-11:

> [9] Therefore God has highly exalted him and bestowed on him the name that is above every name, [10] so that at the name of Jesus every knee should bow, in heaven and on earth and under the earth, [11] and every tongue confess that Jesus Christ is Lord, to the glory of God the Father.

One day every knee will bow before Jesus because He is the "name that is above every name." Therefore, simply by the power of His name, we will all bow on our knees.

Every believer will then stand before the judgment seat of Christ. At this judgment, Christians will be rewarded based on the life that they lived for Jesus. We will not have to pay for our sins at this judgment because Jesus already paid for them at the cross. However, our lives will be evaluated, and our failures will detract from our eternal rewards.

Paul warned us all of this day in 1 Corinthians 3:12-15:

> [12] Now if anyone builds on the foundation with gold, silver, precious stones, wood, hay, straw – [13] each one's

work will become manifest, for the Day will disclose it, because it will be revealed by fire, and the fire will test what sort of work each one has done. [14] If the work that anyone has built on the foundation survives, he will receive a reward. [15] If anyone's work is burned up, he will suffer loss, though he himself will be saved, but only as through fire.

John's statement in today's Scripture correlates with Paul's belief of judgment day for the believer. One day we will all bow before Jesus, who is perfectly pure. When that day comes, each one of us will rejoice for every time we did not give in to temptation. One day it will matter how we approach holiness in our lives.

You cannot truly hope for that day without realizing what will happen when that day comes. In light of these facts, John tells us that true hope leads to pure lives.

Questions:

1. 1 John 1 taught us that God cleanses us from all unrighteousness when we confess our sins.

1 John 1:9 (ESV)
[9] If we confess our sins, he is faithful and just to forgive us our sins and to cleanse us from all unrighteousness.

Today's Scripture says that a person is also to purify himself or herself as Christ is pure. In what ways can you purify yourself?

2. After studying John's words in his first letter up to this point, how would you answer the following question?

What is the goal of pursuing a pure life?

3. How does your hope connect to the pursuit of purity in your life?

Day Twenty-Seven

The Letters of John

Sin is Lawlessness

Sin is not just breaking God's laws;
it is breaking His heart.
Adrian Rogers[1]

Text: 1 John 3:4-6
[4] Everyone who makes a practice of sinning also practices lawlessness; sin is lawlessness. [5] You know that he appeared in order to take away sins, and in him there is no sin. [6] No one who abides in him keeps on sinning; no one who keeps on sinning has either seen him or known him.

Thoughts:
John says that "sin is lawlessness." In other words, everyone who sins breaks the law. Every time we sin, we break a law that God has made. Sin always violates His standards. Therefore, every sin is an act of lawlessness.

Wesleyan scholars David Case and David Holdren give the following explanation for John's statement that "sin is lawlessness":

In this one statement, the writer uses two Greek terms, *hamartia* and *anomia,* to describe aspects of sin. This statement helps us discuss and deal with sin because it gives a clear understanding of what John meant by "sin" or *hamartia.* For John, sin did not include mistakes and human blunders. It is true that some of the Greek words translated "sin" suggest a wide scope of weaknesses, misdirection, and wrongdoing – but not in this epistle. When the writer references the term most often used for sin, that is *hamartia,* he is writing about lawlessness. For him, the sin of greatest concern is the inclination, the attitude, the conscious, rebellious determination to do what is wrong.

This rebellious sin is the kind for which there is clear and full deliverance in this life. A person does not need to live a lifetime with the heart of a rebel. In the partnership of consecration and cleansing, where we come together with God, a person can become brand new in intention, attitude, and behavior. Our consecration or full surrender to God (Romans 12:1) is the beginning of a whole new journey with God in sanctification. We can forever leave behind that "in your face" attitude and replace it with a deep and abiding desire for what God wants for our lives. This is the way to live. The cleansing of the sin nature is a portion of the great theology of holiness.[2]

After clearly stating that sin is lawlessness, John reminds his readers of a truth they already knew: "Jesus Christ appeared to take away sins." (1 John 3:5). "Take away" is the same verb used by John the Baptist when he saw Jesus and proclaimed "Behold, the Lamb of God who takes away the sin of the world!" (John 1:29b) In 1 John 2:28 and 3:2, John uses the word "appears" to refer to the Second Coming of Jesus Christ. Here, in verse 5, he uses it to refer to His first coming. Jesus Christ did not come to this earth primarily to give us moral teaching or an example, although He did those things. His main reason for coming was to take away our sins by paying the penalty that we deserved in His own body on the cross.

The only way that Jesus could pay for our sins and satisfy what God required was to be completely sinless Himself. So, John adds, ". . . and in Him there is no sin." Jesus' virgin birth through the Holy Spirit saved Him from original sin (Luke 1:35). He lived in complete obedience to God, so that even His enemies could find no fault in Him (John 8:46). He offered Himself as a spotless lamb on the sacrificial altar of a wooden cross (1 Peter 1:19). His sacrifice would be the final and complete sacrifice for our sins (Hebrews 10:10-18).

If you know these truths, then John's conclusion in 1 John 3:6 is inescapable:

> [6] No one who abides in him keeps on sinning; no one who keeps on sinning has either seen him or known him.

Questions:

1. What are your thoughts on the phrase "practicing lawlessness" when it comes to your sin? Why is John's phrase, "no one who keeps on sinning" in 1 John 3:6 so important?

2. How does the understanding of sin from the word *hamartia*, "to miss the mark," explain your sinful nature?

3. In what ways have you witnessed Jesus taking your sins away?

Day Twenty-Eight

The Letters of John

Evidence of Being a Child of God

It is not convincing to say you are a child of God
if you have none of the characteristics of your Father.
Kevin DeYoung [1]

Sin and the child of God are incompatible.
They may occasionally meet,
but they cannot live together in harmony.
John Stott [2]

Text: 1 John 3:7-10
[7] Little children, let no one deceive you. Whoever practices righteousness is righteous, as he is righteous. [8] Whoever makes a practice of sinning is of the devil, for the devil has been sinning from the beginning. The reason the Son of God appeared was to destroy the works of the devil. [9] No one born of God makes a practice of sinning, for God's seed abides in him; and he cannot keep on sinning, because he has been born of God. [10] By this it is evident who are the children of God, and who are the children of the devil: whoever does not practice righteousness is not of God, nor is the one who does not love his brother.

Thoughts:
John gives three signs that a person is a saved child of God.

Saved people do not practice sinning, they do practice righteousness, and they love their brothers.

David L. Allen does an excellent job of explaining these proofs of salvation in his commentary, *1–3 John: Fellowship in God's Family*:

> Verse 7 provides the obverse scenario of verse 6: "Whoever practices righteousness is righteous, just as Jesus is righteous." John couches this assertion in a tender pastoral tone: "Little children, let no one deceive you." False teachers are behind the notion that one can be born again and yet practice a sinful lifestyle. John refutes such attempted deception. F.W. Farrar, in *Truths to Live By*, makes this profound statement: "We do not attach ourselves to Christ by our own righteous acts; but because we are attached to Christ, we are able to perform righteous acts. We do not make ourselves God's children because we are good; but being the children of a good God, we can live as His children."
>
> Imagine a professional football player who is an all-pro and master of his position. He knows what his responsibilities are and how to carry out his assignments. Normally, he performs his tasks as he should. But occasionally, he misses an assignment. He may miss a block or a tackle. But that is not the norm for him. Rather, it is the exception. That is the way it is in our Christian life. Sin is the exception, not the rule. If sin is the rule rather than the exception, you have not been born of God.
>
> In verse 8, John carries the trajectory of his argument even further. He tracks the source of habitual sin to Satan himself. Jesus made the same connection in John 8:44:

"You are of your father the devil, and your will is to do your father's desires. He was a murderer from the beginning, and does not stand in the truth, because there is no truth in him. When he lies, he speaks out of his own character, for he is a liar and the father of lies."

The name "devil" means "slanderer; accuser." The devil's lifestyle of sin has been so "from the beginning." This probably refers to the beginning of Satan's rebellion against God. John then states why Jesus "appeared" concerning the devil: that he might destroy his works.

John now begins to draw his argument to a close by stating in verse 9 that no one who has been born of God practices sin. His use of the perfect tense stresses the complete and final nature of the new birth. The reason why the Christian cannot practice sin is because he has been given new birth by God himself. The crucial question is, what does John mean by the phrase "God's seed"? John is referring to the fact of the divine nature in us by virtue of the new birth. This new birth prohibits a lifestyle of sin in one who is truly born again. Christians may sin, as John has already confirmed in his letter (1:5–10). But genuine Christians don't want to sin.

John's final point is found in verse 10. Every person is a member of one of two families: God's family or the devil's family. The distinguishing mark is what one practices: righteousness or sin. One who does not practice righteousness is not "of God," meaning God is not his spiritual Father. The foolproof test in this paternity dispute is to take swabs of lifestyle, and the one that shows no evidence of someone doing the right thing can't be God's child.

John then adds a final comment specifying one act of righteousness that he has already addressed and will address again: loving Christian brothers and sisters in the church.

In essence, God and Satan are the heads of two families. You are either a child of God or of Satan. Every person who has not been born into the family of God is a member of the family of Satan. The new birth determines what family you are in today.[3]

Questions:

1. How are you doing on the three proofs of being a child of God?

God's children do not practice sinning.

God's children practice righteousness.

God's children love their brothers and sisters in Christ.

2. Which one causes you the most difficulty in your daily walk?

3. As His child, in what ways do you resemble your Heavenly Father?

Day Twenty-Nine

The Letters of John

The Message of Love

More people have been brought into the church by the kindness of real Christian love than by all the theological arguments in the world, and more people have been driven from the church by the hardness and ugliness of so-called Christianity than by all the doubts in the world.
William Barclay[1]

Text: 1 John 3:11
[11] For this is the message that you have heard from the beginning, that we should love one another.

Thoughts:
The apostle John spoke often about the message of love. The word "love" occurs forty-six times in 1 John. In addition, it appears fifty-seven times in the Gospel of John, more often than in the other three Gospels combined. 1 John 3:11 brings us again to the focus of love in a believer's life.

The first part of today's Scripture, "For this is the message that you have heard from the beginning," is very similar to the following verses:

1 John 1:5a (ESV)
[5a] This is the message we have heard from him and proclaim to you...

1 John 2:7 (ESV)

⁷ Beloved, I am writing you no new commandment, but an old commandment that you had from the beginning. The old commandment is the word that you have heard.

Today's verse reminds John's readers of a specific command that had been handed down within the community of Christ-followers. John specifically calls it the "message" they had heard from the beginning. The term "message" comes from the Greek word *angelia*, which means "to announce." God has announced His message loud and clear: love one another.

John is reminding his readers to obey the commandment that they had already heard. It is one thing to believe what God says. It is another thing altogether to obey it. David Allen addresses this truth in his commentary on 1 John:

> It is not enough to believe rightly. We must behave rightly. Being precedes doing, but all Christian doing must be based on being, that is, on who we are in Christ. Our practice proclaims who and what we are.[2]

John often repeated the message of God's love. He devotes a major portion of the next chapter of 1 John to this crucial message (1 John 4:7-21). Stephen Cole, in his writings on 1 John, shares these important words regarding John's message of love:

> John had seen the love of Christ demonstrated that night in the Upper Room, when Jesus took the basin of water and washed the disciples' feet. He then heard Jesus say (John 13:34–35), "A new commandment I give to you, that you love one another, even as I have loved

you, that you also love one another. By this all men will know that you are My disciples, if you have love for one another." Then John saw the supreme demonstration of Christ's love when He willingly went to the cross to die for our sins. And so the "son of thunder" became known as the "apostle of love."

If we get weary of hearing over and over about the need to love one another, we should remember that John wrote under the inspiration of the Holy Spirit, who knows our hearts. We need to examine ourselves constantly because our default mode is to revert to selfishness, not to love.[3]

May we continue to heed the announcement "love one another," and keep focusing on constantly showing God's love to those around us.

Questions:

1. Why do you think the Holy Spirit inspired writers of Scripture to repeat the theme of "loving one another" so often?

2. In what tangible ways can you show that you love others with the love of Jesus Christ?

3. How can you keep announcing the message to other believers? Think of one way you can lovingly encourage others to express God's love to other people.

Day Thirty

The Letters of John

The Ultimate Contrast

A person's life is his most precious possession. Consequently, to rob him of it is the greatest sin we can commit against him, while to give one's life on his behalf is the greatest possible expression of love for him (1 John 3:16). This, then, is the ultimate contrast: Cain's hatred issued in murder, Christ's love issued in self-sacrifice.

John Stott[1]

Text: 1 John 3:12-16

[12] We should not be like Cain, who was of the evil one and murdered his brother. And why did he murder him? Because his own deeds were evil and his brother's righteous. [13] Do not be surprised, brothers, that the world hates you. [14] We know that we have passed out of death into life, because we love the brothers. Whoever does not love abides in death. [15] Everyone who hates his brother is a murderer, and you know that no murderer has eternal life abiding in him. [16] By this we know love, that he laid down his life for us, and we ought to lay down our lives for the brothers.

Thoughts:

John has a unique style of writing that reveals both sides of a situation. He has the divine ability to give us the difference between real Christianity and false religion. It is no surprise, then, that his first letter is full of contrasts. Here is a summary of the contrasts we have seen thus far in 1 John:

Light / Darkness	1 John 1:5
New Command / Old Command	1 John 2:7-8
Loving God / Loving the world	1 John 2:15-16
Christ / Antichrist	1 John 2:18-22
Truth / Lies	1 John 2:20-21
Children of God / Children of the Devil	1 John 3:1-10

1 John 3:12-16 gives us the ultimate contrast of love and hatred. Stephen Cole provides a greater understanding into this contrast of hatred and love found in today's Scripture:

> In our text, John again gets out his black and white paint and does not mix them into shades of gray. He wants to expose the errors of the heretics in the plainest of terms. So he contrasts the world with the church. His message is, "The mark of the world is hatred, but the mark of the church is love."
>
> **The mark of the world is hatred.**
> Sometimes to define a somewhat vague notion like love it is helpful to contrast it with the opposite, hatred. So John contrasts the love that we are to have for one another with Cain's murder of his brother, Abel (3:11–12). Then, he states (3:13), "Do not be surprised, brethren, if the world hates you."
>
> John here reflects Jesus' words in the Upper Room (John 15:18–19 [see also, John 17:14]), "If the world hates you, you know that it has hated Me before it hated you. If you were of the world, the world would love its own; but because you are not of the world, but I

chose you out of the world, because of this the world hates you."

By *the world*, John means the unbelieving world, of course, which is under Satan's dominion in opposition to God. But, in particular, John was targeting those who had left the church and were promoting false teaching about the person and work of Christ.

When John speaks of *love*, he points us to the supreme example of Jesus laying down His life for us (3:16). Thus a helpful definition of biblical love is: *a self-sacrificing, caring commitment that shows itself in seeking the highest good of the one loved.* Jesus sacrificed Himself because He cared for us and He is committed to seek our highest good, that ultimately, we might share His glory.

Since hatred is the opposite of love, we may define it as, *a selfish, insensitive attitude that shows itself in disregarding others' good as I seek my own interests.* The essence of hatred is the self-centered bent of fallen human nature that says, "I'll help you if it helps me or if it's not too much of a hassle. But if it comes down to you or me, I'm looking out for me!" When we understand hatred as such, we can see that it characterizes the unbelieving world. The world is motivated by self-interest. Self-sacrifice, to the world, is crazy.

The mark of the church is love.

John draws a sharp contrast between the hatred that marks the world and the love that marks the church. Whereas hatred is typified in Adam's firstborn, love is typified in God's firstborn, Christ (1 John 3:16).

Verse 16 literally reads, "By this we have experientially come to know love, that One laid down His life for us." The cross is the supreme demonstration of what real love – God's love – is. There is hardly a passage in the New Testament that speaks of God's love that does not also speak of the cross. The most familiar is another 3:16: "For God so loved the world, that He gave His only begotten Son, that whoever believes in Him should not perish, but have eternal life." (See, also, Gal. 2:20; Rom. 5:8; Eph. 5:25; 1 John 4:10.) If you want to know what God's love is like, look at Jesus, the Righteous One, who willingly sacrificed Himself on behalf of the ungodly.

Whereas hatred originates with the devil, love originates with God.

John will state this directly in 1 John 4:7, but it is implicit in our text. Love in the believer comes from God. In 1 John 3:10b, John said that the one who does not love is not of God, implying that the one who loves is of God. In 1 John 3:17, he says that if we do not demonstrate practical love for those in need, the love of God does not abide in us. If you lack love for someone, first make sure that you are born of God. Then, ask Him for it.

Whereas hatred divides people and may result in murder, love unites people and results in laying down our lives for others (1 John 3:16).[2]

Questions:

1. In what ways do you bear the mark of the world: hatred?

2. In what ways do you bear the mark of the church: love?

3. How does the extreme contrast between hatred and love found in today's Scripture help you to draw closer to Christ?

Day Thirty-One

The Letters of John

Love in Action

Beware that you are not swallowed up in books.
An ounce of love is worth a pound of knowledge.
John Wesley [1]

Text: 1 John 3:17-18
[17] But if anyone has the world's goods and sees his brother in need, yet closes his heart against him, how does God's love abide in him? [18] Little children, let us not love in word or talk but in deed and in truth.

Thoughts:
Yesterday, we looked at the great contrast between hatred and love, while we read these words in 1 John 3:16: "By this we know love, that he laid down his life for us, and we ought to lay down our lives for the brothers." Right after John challenges us that true Christian love means being willing to lay our lives down, he confronts us with this question in 1 John 3:17: "But if anyone has the world's goods and sees his brother in need, yet closes his heart against him, how does God's love abide in him?" We may never be called upon to lay our lives down, but all of us can respond in love to the needs of others.

Every time we see a need, our Christian love is tested. Will we respond with action, or will we close our hearts against the person in need? If we have been blessed with resources to help, God has already placed His love in our hearts to respond.

John follows up his challenging questions with a call to action in 1 John 3:18: ". . . let us not love in word or talk, but in deed and in truth."

In essence, John is saying, "Talk is cheap." We are not to talk about how much we love everybody and our concern for them.

We are not to love in tongue or with insincerity. We are put our love into action. We are to love in deed, and doing so may require sacrifice.

Look through the Bible, and you find a number of examples of people who loved in deed, including Jesus. There were three Hebrew men who would rather die than disobey God. Daniel loved God so much that he was willing to die rather than stop praying to the Lord and pray to someone else. The Macedonian Christians gave sacrificially to Paul's ministry so the gospel could be spread to the lost. Ruth followed and served Naomi when she did not have to do this. David's mighty men loved him and were willing to give their lives in battle as they fought with him.

John said that we are to love in deed. We are to love in truth or sincerity. Our love is to be genuine and not fake. This was a problem in John's day as well as in our own age. If your life is going to be a living message that impacts others, then your love for God and people must be genuine and be demonstrated in your life by what you do as well as what you say.

Questions:

1. How does seeing a need lead to a response of love in the life of a believer?

2. If your heart is open to Jesus, how can it be closed to the needs of those around you?

3. Mother Teresa once made the following statement concerning love in action:

> "When you know how much God is in love with you, then you can only live your life radiating that love."

What are your thoughts on her statement?

Day Thirty-Two

The Letters of John

Love Reassures Our Hearts Before God

The height of our love for God
will never exceed the depth of our love for one another.
Patrick Morley[1]

Text: 1 John 3:19-20
[19] By this we shall know that we are of the truth and reassure
our heart before him; [20] for whenever our heart condemns us,
God is greater than our heart, and he knows everything.

Thoughts:

Love is like a multifaceted diamond. As we have seen in
our study, love reflects the level of our abiding in Christ. In
addition, John has placed love against the dark backdrop of
hate and shown us the ultimate contrast. Yesterday, we were
given a reminder in 1 John 3:18 that divine love involves action: "Little children, let us not love in word or talk but in
deed and in truth."

As John continues in his first epistle, he reveals another
multi-sided truth about love. Love reflects its truth in action and
reassures our hearts before God. The beginning of 1 John 3:19
can be translated: "Hereby we know that we are truly His . . ."
The display of love divulges the true nature of our hearts. When
the love of Christ is revealed through our actions, we gain assurance that His love truly resides in our lives.

The Christian life isn't easy. As we seek to grow closer to Christ, we still struggle with the attacks of the devil. The evil one often attacks our thoughts regarding the assurance of our salvation. Verses 19-20 can provide us security in our salvation and give us victory over the battle going on in our hearts.

David Case and David Holdren, in *A Commentary for Bible Students*, give the following insight:

> It is not unusual to encounter personal doubt and self-condemnation. The doubts may be part of one's spiritual struggle in relation to God or the struggle may be self-doubt. The context for verses 19-20 is captured in the words **whenever our hearts condemn us** (3:20). The writer *expects* those inner attacks to occur. Some people spend enormous amounts of their lives being consumed by feelings of self-condemnation. Such feelings adversely transform our perspective, alter our moods, and can incline us to under-respond and over-react. But God understands. God also provides help in such times of need. God's Word and Spirit offer healing and hope. We need that healing and hope, and we need to offer it to others.[2]

Questions:

1. Have you struggled with doubt regarding your salvation? What have you learned today that can help you be more secure in your relationship with God?

2. The devil always deals in condemnation while God brings conviction. How does the phrase, "God is greater than our heart and He knows everything" bring comfort to your struggle today?

3. Take a minute today and evaluate the love displayed through your words and actions. Ask God to reveal the truth about where you are spiritually and write down your response.

Day Thirty-Three

The Letters of John

A Commandment About Faith and Love

The two chief things are faith and love.
Faith receives the good; love gives the good.
Faith offers us God as our own;
love gives us to our neighbor as His own.
Martin Luther [1]

Text: 1 John 3:21-24

[21] Beloved, if our heart does not condemn us, we have confidence before God; [22] and whatever we ask we receive from him, because we keep his commandments and do what pleases him. [23] And this is his commandment, that we believe in the name of his Son Jesus Christ and love one another, just as he has commanded us. [24] Whoever keeps his commandments abides in God, and God in him. And by this we know that he abides in us, by the Spirit whom he has given us.

Thoughts:

Over the last few days, John has taught us that our love for God displayed through our actions can bring us assurance about what we truly believe in our hearts. God desires to bring us to victory over our struggle with doubts. As we look closely at our own lives realizing God knows everything about our hearts, we can trust God to bring us to a place of confidence in our relationship with Him.

Confident assurance in our salvation dramatically changes the approach to our Christian life. When we know we are saved, we can pray with confidence. When we are obeying God's commands out of our genuine love for Him, we know we are growing closer to Him. The closer we grow to Him personally, the more power we feel in our conversations with Him.

When you love your heavenly Father with all of your heart, it changes your perspective of His commands. Rather than seeing His commands as restrictive, you begin to understand that His commands are there for your protection and direction. God wants you to experience the victorious life, so He gives you commands in order to guide you there safely. This leads us to the two commandments found in 1 John 3:23: "And this is his commandment, that we believe in the name of his Son Jesus Christ and love one another, just as he has commanded us." These commandments center around our faith and love. God commands us to believe in Him and love one another because He knows that faith and love are directly related to each other. When we believe in Him fully, we love one another freely. In addition, our love for one another reveals how much we believe in Him. So faith and love have an incredible correlation to our connection to Jesus Christ.

John adds to this connection of faith and love in verse 24: "Whoever keeps his commandments abides in God, and God in him . . ." Did you see the dual direction again of faith and love? If you keep God's commandments, you know you abide in Him. If you have faith and love, you also know God abides in you.

On top of that, John closes verse 24 with: ". . . And by this we know that he abides in us, by the Spirit whom he has given us." God not only sent His son, He also sent His Spirit. Both were sent out of God's deep desire for us to be saved and to know it. His commands concerning faith and love, combined with the presence of His Spirit, show us God's intense longing for us to live confidently in our walk with the Lord.

Questions:

1. Have you had the wrong view of God's commands in your life? In what ways? How should you properly view His commands?

2. Do you see faith and love working together in your spiritual journey?

3. What does God's desire for your security reveal about His deep love for you?

Day Thirty-Four

The Letters of John

Test Everything

[19] Do not quench the Spirit.
[20] Do not despise prophecies,
[21] but test everything; hold fast what is good.
[22] Abstain from every form of evil.
1 Thessalonians 5:19-22

Text: 1 John 4:1-3

[1] Beloved, do not believe every spirit, but test the spirits to see whether they are from God, for many false prophets have gone out into the world. [2] By this you know the Spirit of God: every spirit that confesses that Jesus Christ has come in the flesh is from God, [3] and every spirit that does not confess Jesus is not from God. This is the spirit of the antichrist, which you heard was coming and now is in the world already.

Thoughts:

For centuries mankind has been looking for an effective way to discern the truth from a lie. In the early 1700s, there was a theory that someone's pulse could be used to determine if they were lying. In 1892, James Mackenzie was credited with inventing the lie detector, known as a polygraph. The word polygraph comes from two Greek words: *poly*, which means "many," and *graph*, which denotes "writings." The "many writings" refer to all that a polygraph records, such as heart rate, blood pressure, perspiration, respiration, and skin conductivity. Even with all the years of fine tuning, a polygraph is admissible as evidence of guilt in a criminal trial in less than half of the states in the U.S.

Today's Scripture reveal God's test for determining truth. John tells us to "test the spirits to see whether they are from God. . ."

> John warned against believing **every spirit**; that is, we are never to assume every spiritual experience or every demonstration of spiritual power is from God. We must test spiritual experiences and spiritual phenomena to see if they are, in fact, from God. This is important because **many false prophets have gone out into the world**. Even though the early church had a strong life and a large measure of purity, John still knew the danger false prophets and their message brought to the early church.[1]

The word John uses for "test" in verse 1 is the Greek word *dokimazo*. This word means "to put to the test in order to approve." This word was used to describe the testing of metals to determine whether or not they were genuine. *Dokimazo* is the same word used in 1 Thessalonians 5:21: "test everything; hold fast what is good." It is also used in a warning not to take the Lord's Supper in an unworthy manner found in 1 Corinthians 11:28: "Let a person examine himself, then, and so eat of the bread and drink of the cup."

In 1 John 4:2-3, John gives one sure way to know that something is from the Spirit of God: ". . . every spirit that confesses that Jesus Christ has come in the flesh is from God, and every spirit that does not confess Jesus is not from God."

128

Curtis Vaughan, in the *Founders Study Guide Commentary*, explains this test as follows:

> The crux of it is the rejection or acceptance of Jesus Christ as the incarnate Son of God. "Every spirit that confesses" is a reference to prophetic utterances made under the claim of divine inspiration. The essence of the confession is "that Jesus Christ has come in the flesh." In it there is a great truth implied (the preexistence of Christ) and a great truth asserted (Christ's real incarnation). From this we gather that the crucial matter in testing the spirits is to determine the attitude of the prophet toward Jesus Christ. No prophetic utterance is to be received as coming from the Spirit of God if that utterance does not acknowledge Jesus Christ to be the incarnate Son of God.[2]

Questions:

1. Have you seen people deceived by lies from false prophets? Why is this section of Scripture so critical to the preservation of the truth about Jesus Christ?

2. How does truth expose lies when it comes to your spiritual journey?

3. How does the examination of your own heart tie into your ability to test what other people say about Jesus?

Day Thirty-Five

The Letters of John

He Is Greater

It's not great faith you need; it is faith in a great God.
N.T. Wright[1]

When God says something, the argument is over.
R.C. Sproul[2]

Text: 1 John 4:4-6
[4] Little children, you are from God and have overcome them, for he who is in you is greater than he who is in the world. [5] They are from the world; therefore they speak from the world, and the world listens to them. [6] We are from God. Whoever knows God listens to us; whoever is not from God does not listen to us. By this we know the Spirit of truth and the spirit of error.

Thoughts:

After John told believers to test the spirits, he reminded them of the power of Christ who lived in them. These words from John provide great encouragement but are difficult to explain. For today's devotion, we will depend on some well-versed theologians to gain a better understanding and application of today's Scripture:

The *Life Application Bible Commentary* adds this profound insight:

Some Christians want to do this spiritual battle as individuals. They take "he who is in *you*" as "he who is in *me*." But the pronoun is plural, thus referring to the community of believers. Believers do have personal assurance of the Holy Spirit's presence within. But they must not attempt to do battle against Satan alone. They need others for prayer, resources, advice, guidance, protection, healing, and more.[4]

John Stott's commentary explains how 1 John 4:5-6 connect to the previous four verses of 1 John 4:

> These two verses are complementary. In them John contrasts in striking fashion not only the false prophets and the true apostles (*they* and *we*), but the different audiences who listen to them, namely *the world* and *whoever knows God*. The world recognizes its own people and listens to their message, which originates in its own circle and reflects its own perspectives. This explains their popularity.
>
> *We*, on the other hand, *are from God*. The *we* of this verse is in direct antithesis to the *they* of the previous verse. So, if *they* means the false teachers, *we* must mean the true teachers, namely the apostles. But how can it be known that *we are from God* and are teaching the truth? You can tell that our message is God's message, John explains, because God's people listen to it and receive it. This statement sounds the height of arrogance. So it would be if uttered by an individual Christian. No private believer could presume to say: 'whoever knows God agrees with me; only those who are not from God disagree with me.' But this is what John says. For he is writing in the name neither of himself nor of the church, but of Christ, as one of his chosen apostles.

He is carrying a step further the argument of the first three verses of 1 John 4. There the test of doctrine was whether it acknowledged the divine-human person of Jesus Christ; here the test is whether it is accepted by Christians and rejected by non-Christians. There is a certain affinity between God's Word and God's people. Jesus had taught that his sheep hear his voice (John 10:4–5, 8, 16, 26–27), that everyone who is on the side of truth listens to his witness to the truth (John 18:37), and that 'he who belongs to God hears what God says' (John 8:47). In the same way John asserts that since *we are from God* (vs. 6) and 'you . . . are from God' (vs. 4), you listen to us. There is a correspondence between the message and hearers.[5]

Questions:

1. In what ways are you tempted to live your Christian life in isolation? Why is it important that the "you" is plural in "He who is in you"?

2. How can the worldwide church do a better job of uniting to expose the Spirit of truth? What part can you play in living towards unity around the truth of God's Word?

3. How do you rely on the greatness of Christ in you to discern the Spirit of truth from the spirit of error?

Day Thirty-Six

The Letters of John

God Is Love

A Christian is hopelessly in love with Jesus,
and helplessly dependent on Him.
Maxie Dunnam [1]

Text: 1 John 4:7-8
[7] Beloved, let us love one another, for love is from God, and whoever loves has been born of God and knows God. [8] Anyone who does not love does not know God, because God is love.

Thoughts:
David Allen, in *Preaching the Word* commentary, gives an insightful introduction to this portion of Scripture:

> Dozens of times in this letter alone John uses the word "love." Primarily he speaks about three kinds of love: God's love for us, our love for God, and our love for one another. The concept of love is so important to John that three times he discusses it in this letter. This is the third passage. The first time was in chapter 2, he talked about love as evidence for our fellowship with God. In chapter 3 it was the evidence of our sonship with God. Now in chapter 4, John comes to the apex of what love is. He traces the stream of love to its source: "God is love." [2]

1 John 4:7 was an extremely important verse of Scripture in John's life:

> The church father, Jerome, said that when the apostle John was in his extreme old age, he was so weak that he had to be carried into the church meetings. At the end of the meeting, he would be helped to his feet to give a word of exhortation to the church. Invariably, he would repeat, "Little children, let us love one another." John's disciples began to grow weary of the same words every time, and they finally asked him why he always said the same thing over and over. He replied, "Because it is the Lord's commandment, and if this only is done, it is enough."[3]

> Regarding verse 8, John Wesley said, "This little sentence brought John more sweetness, even in the time he was writing it, than the whole world can bring."[4]

Some of the greatest truths found in all of Scripture are found in 1 John 4:7-8. God is love. It is in His very nature to love. Divine love comes straight from our divine God because love is who He is. Love doesn't just describe His actions; it depicts His essence. Bees can't help but buzz. Birds can't help but fly. God cannot help but love because that is who He is.

Everyone that God commands to love can know for certain that they are loved by God. We have the ability to love others given to us by a God who loves us and who is love Himself. David Allen says, "Our love is not an imitation from a distance but participation from within."[5] Because God is love and He loves us and lives in us, we have the divine ability within us to love one another.

John states that there are two things that are true about Christians who practice love: they have been born of God and they know God. David Allen explains these two realities as follows:

> The presence of love in your life is an evidence of your Christian experience. Of course, John does not mean that anybody in the world who has a feeling of love for somebody else is therefore a Christian. John is talking about the relationship between God and believers. If you have children, they possess your DNA. Your children have your nature, which has been genetically passed on to them. John is saying that a similar thing is true of those who have been born of God. If God as to his nature is love, then everyone who has truly been born of God partakes of his nature of love. Not only have we been born of God, but a second thing is true about us: we know God. The word "knows" here conveys the meaning of having an intimate relationship with God. It is more than knowing facts about God or understanding perceived truths about God. To know God really means to be rightly related to him.[6]

Questions:

1. Why do you think 1 John 4:7 and the biblical concept of love meant so much to the beloved disciple John?

2. What does it mean to you that God is love?

3. How does your love for others demonstrate your spiritual birth and your true knowledge of God?

4. How does Maxie Dunnam's quote that began today's devotion apply to your life and this lesson today?

Day Thirty-Seven

The Letters of John

Love Manifested

God loves each of us as if there were only one of us.
Saint Augustine[1]

Nothing binds me to my Lord
like a strong belief in His changeless love.
Charles H. Spurgeon[2]

Text: 1 John 4:9-10
[9] In this the love of God was made manifest among us, that God sent his only Son into the world, so that we might live through him. [10] In this is love, not that we have loved God but that he loved us and sent his Son to be the propitiation for our sins.

Thoughts:
God's love was manifested when He sent His Son. When our invisible God sent His only Son visibly into the world, we got a plain view of God's magnificent love. The word "manifested" means "to become apparent" or "graspable." The love of God was proven when He sent Jesus to die for our sins. Jesus' sacrifice on the cross not only satisfied our sin debt, but it showed the depth of God's love for us. We have the power to live through Christ because God had the passion to send His Son.

Ben Witherington shared the following stories that illustrate the truth about God's manifested love:

There is an old hymn written by a man whose last name is Lehman. The most memorable verse of this hymn was the last thing Mr. Lehman ever wrote, for it was found scrawled on the padded wall of his cell, in which he was found dead. It reads as follows:

"The love of God is greater far than tongue or pen can tell; it goes beyond the highest star and reaches lowest hell. Could we with ink the ocean fill, and were the skies a parchment made, were every stalk on earth a quill and every man a scribe by trade, to write the love of God above would drain the ocean dry. Nor could the scroll contain the whole if stretched across the sky."

Victor Furnish, one of the great NT scholars of our era has put the matter in this fashion – 'God's love is not like a heat-seeking missile which is triggered by something inherently attractive in the target, the object of love'. Indeed not, God loves us when we are unlovely, indeed in some respects seemingly unlovable. God loves us whether we love God back or not. God's love is unconditional, in the sense that it is given freely, and not because of anything we have said or done or felt. Indeed, God's love is often given in spite of what we have said or done or felt. It is pure grace – God's unmerited favor, God's undeserved, unearned benefit freely and lavishly poured out by God into our lives.[3]

Questions:

1. What significance does John's use of the phrase "in this," found at the beginning of both verses for our study today, bring to the concept of God's love?

2. What other Scriptures come to mind when you consider how much God loves you?

3. What did you learn today about God's love from Ben Witherington's two illustrations?

Day Thirty-Eight

The Letters of John

His Love is Perfected in Us

God's love for me is perfect because it's based on Him
not on me. So even when I fail, He keeps loving me.
Anonymous

Text: 1 John 4:11-12
[11] Beloved, if God so loved us, we also ought to love one another. [12] No one has ever seen God; if we love one another, God abides in us and his love is perfected in us.

Thoughts:

John, the beloved disciple, refers to God's children as the "beloved." The word "beloved" in the Greek is an adjective form of the verb *agape*. *Agape* is the highest form of love because it the love that God has for us. One option of translation for the word "beloved" is "loved by God." John places a double emphasis on God's love for us as he begins verse 11. He essentially states: "Those loved by God, we ought to love one another since God so loved us."

John Stott, in *The Letters of John: An Introduction and Commentary*, provides great insight to 1 John 4:11:

The historical manifestation of God's love in Christ not only assures us of his love for us, but lays upon us the obligation to love one another. No one who has been to the cross and seen God's immeasurable and unmerited love displayed there can go back to a life of selfishness. Indeed, the implication seems to be that our love should resemble his love: *since God so loved us, we also ought* – in like manner and to a like degree of self-sacrifice - *to love one another*. The duty of Christian self-sacrifice is deduced from the self-sacrifice of Christ.[1]

Rick Williamson, in *A Commentary in the Wesleyan Tradition*, gives a great explanation of 1 John 4:12:

That God is unseen is a consistent biblical emphasis. An identical statement appears in John 1:18: **No one has ever seen God**. Exodus 33:20 is representative of Old Testament teaching. There the Lord told Moses, "You cannot see my face, for no one may see me and live." The New Testament describes God as "invisible" (1 Timothy 1:17 and Hebrews 11:27).

The perfect tense of **has ... seen** stresses that God was not seen in the past and continues to be unseen in the present. Although no one can directly see God, God is knowable to some extent since He lives in us as we live out His love for others. Love from God, incarnate in followers of Jesus, powerfully demonstrates God's purpose in the world.

Even if God cannot be seen directly as gnostic heretics thought, God can be seen when his people act in love. John insists that divine love infused into us can be perfected. That is, it fulfills its purpose or achieves its end, among us as we live in love. His love is made complete. This verb shows that God brings us to the goal He has in mind for us. Christian excellence is not a human achievement based on merit or struggle. It is God graciously at work, achieving His intentions for us as we love one another.[2]

Through the Holy Spirit's presence, God resides in every believer. Currently, Jesus cannot be seen on Earth in a bodily form because He is seated at the right hand of God's throne (Hebrews 12:2). However, Christ can be seen through the love that believers show for one another. As the love of God develops and matures in the lives of growing Christians, His love is made complete through His children.

Questions:

1. Are you prone to forgetting that in Christ, you are beloved? How can knowing you are constantly loved by God give you more consistency in your love for others?

2. How can you trust God to perfect His love in you while you continue to work out your salvation with fear and trembling? In other words, how do you work out your salvation while God continues to perfect His love through your life?

3. In what ways are you challenged and convicted knowing that the world can see Christ through your Christian love for other people?

Day Thirty-Nine

The Letters of John

Abiding in Him and He in Us

On the whole, God's love for us is a much safer subject
to think about than our love for Him.
C. S. Lewis

Text: 1 John 4:13-17

¹³ By this we know that we abide in him and he in us, because
he has given us of his Spirit. ¹⁴ And we have seen and testify
that the Father has sent his Son to be the Savior of the world.
¹⁵ Whoever confesses that Jesus is the Son of God, God abides in
him, and he in God. ¹⁶ So we have come to know and to believe
the love that God has for us. God is love, and whoever abides
in love abides in God, and God abides in him. ¹⁷ By this is love
perfected with us, so that we may have confidence for the day
of judgment, because as he is so also are we in this world.

Thoughts:

David Guzik connects today's Scripture with yesterday's
verses with these insightful remarks concerning verse 13:

By beginning with the words **by this**, John connected
the thought of this verse directly to the previous verse.
We can *know by experience* that we live in God, if *His love
has been perfected in us*. And we know that *His love has
been perfected in us* if we *love one another*.

Plainly, Christians can say, "**We know**." We don't have to merely "hope" we are saved, and "hope" we will make it to heaven, thus having no assurance of salvation before we pass from this world to the next. We can **know**, and we can **know** now, on *this* side of eternity.[1]

Guzik also says we can know we abide in Christ, "…because He has given us of His Spirit."

John brings up the work of the Holy Spirit in us at this point for two important connections. First, it is the Spirit of God in us that is the abiding presence of Jesus— the presence of His Spirit is *how* He abides in us. Secondly, it is the testimony of the Holy Spirit within us that makes it possible for us to **know that we abide in Him**. As Paul puts it in Roman 8:16: "The Spirit Himself bears witness with our spirit that we are children of God." The Holy Spirit gives us this assurance.[2]

The security we have in our relationship with Jesus comes directly from our abiding in God and His abiding in us.

In 1 John 4:14-15, John connects our abiding in Christ to our testimony and confession that Jesus is the Son of God and the Savior of the world. Verse 16 ties our assurance to the faith that we have in God's love for us. Thus, our abiding in Him comes from what we believe about Him that leads to our willingness to testify and confess that Jesus is Lord.

As we consider today the topic of abiding in Christ, may the following illustration encourage you to stay close to the Son:

The planet Mercury is hot. Pluto is cold. Why is Pluto cold and Mercury hot? Mercury is really close to the sun and Pluto is a long way off. The farther you get away, the colder things become, but the closer you get, the hotter things are. You may say that you are not a Pluto Christian or a Mercury Christian. Maybe you are an Earth Christian where things get hot and cold. You may be a seasonal Christian who has changes depending on whether it is wintertime, summertime, springtime, or fall.

God is looking for some Mercury Christians. He is looking for some folks who want to get close and stay hot all the time because they stay close to the SON.[3]

Questions:

1. How does your faith in God, your love for Him and one another, and your obedience to God's commands connect to your abiding in Jesus Christ?

2. How does God abide in you?

3. What tangible ways can you remain faithful to abide in Christ?

Day Forty

The Letters of John

Commanded to Love

Here is a spiritual principle: We cannot exercise love
unless we are experiencing grace. You cannot truly love
others unless you are convinced that God's love for you is
unconditional, based solely on the merit of Christ, not on
your performance. John said, "We love because he first loved
us" (1 John 4:19). Our love, either to God or others, can only
be a response to His love for us.
Jerry Bridges[1]

Text: 1 John 4:18-21
[18] There is no fear in love, but perfect love casts out fear. For fear
has to do with punishment, and whoever fears has not been
perfected in love. [19] We love because he first loved us. [20] If anyone says, "I love God," and hates his brother, he is a liar; for he
who does not love his brother whom he has seen cannot love
God whom he has not seen. [21] And this commandment we have
from him: whoever loves God must also love his brother.

Thoughts:
John begins this section of Scripture with the statement,
"There is no fear in love." *A Commentary for Bible Students*
states:

The immediate context of this verse is focused on our relationship with God and our assurance before Him regarding judgment. John writes, ". . . but perfect love drives out fear, because fear has to do with punishment." When we know that our focus is to love God and others, we take it by faith that such obedience will deliver us. We need not live in fear of God, or in anxiety about our destiny.[2]

We never have to fear when we are loved by the God who created us and will one day judge the world.

John's statement, "We love because he first loved us," gives us our greatest purpose and passion to love others. God's love is a gift that He has given to us. God's love is our reason to return love to others.

John closes out this portion of Scripture on love reminding us that God commands us to love one another.

In a blog post entitled, "The Nature of True Love," Ben Witherington gave the following comments on God's command to love:

Have you noticed that in the Bible we are frequently commanded to love? It should have struck us as odd that love is commanded, if we are used to associating love with mere feelings. Jesus says that love of God and of others is the greatest commandment. He even commands us to love our enemies, which surely does not mean love them to death by killing them. But is he really ordering our feelings to march in lockstep in a particular direction? Have you ever said to your children---- "I demand that for the next three minutes you will feel happy and cheerful!" If you have tried such an experiment of commanding others feelings or even your own, doubtless you have discovered it is an exercise in futility. Feelings cannot be commanded. They come and they go, and they are subject to the fluctuations of life, affected and prompted by a thousand different factors – whether or not we are healthy, whether we are hungry, whether we are sleepy and a host of other factors.

So here is where I tell you that in the Bible love is normally an action word. It refers to a decision of the will that then leads to an action. Most often it refers to an activity, not a feeling at all. [3]

Since love is not a feeling, it can be commanded. Because love is an action, let's go love one another because God first loved us.

Questions:

1. In what ways does perfect love drive out your fears?

2. Why is it reassuring and refreshing to know that "We love because He first loved us"?

3. What are your thoughts on God commanding us to love one another?

Day Forty-One

The Letters of John

A Belief that Is Not a Burden

John was just as concerned about a person's spiritual belief
and spiritual birth as he was about a person's love.
If someone is not a true believer,
he or she has not experienced the new birth.
And if someone has not experienced the new birth,
that person cannot live right nor die right.
John was concerned that a man truly be born again.
James Merritt

Text: 1 John 5:1-3
[1] Everyone who believes that Jesus is the Christ has been born
of God, and everyone who loves the Father loves whoever has
been born of him. [2] By this we know that we love the children of
God, when we love God and obey his commandments.
[3] For this is the love of God, that we keep his commandments.
And his commandments are not burdensome.

Thoughts:
1 John 4:7-21 focused on the love of God that every believer should demonstrate. In 1 John 5, John turns his attention to faith and spiritual birth. Our behavior is determined by our beliefs. In other words, we do what we do because of who we are. If we are born spiritually, we will grow spiritually. The Spirit of God births us into a life that is empowered by God.

If you were like me, I grew up with more religion than relationship. My faith in God was, in all reality, works-based. I did what I did because I was supposed to. If I obeyed God's commandments, I felt better about who I was. I went to church because I thought it would please God more. Everything I did in my early days of what I thought was Christianity was really based on my attempts to be good enough before God to feel good enough about myself.

John was writing to people just like me. He wanted to make sure that they understood that who they were in Christ led to their obedience, not the other way around. Spiritual birth always precedes spiritual fruit. When you have put full faith in Jesus Christ, you realize your Christian life is less about trying, and more about trusting. This doesn't mean you don't develop spiritual disciplines. It simply means your faith is in all that God has already done rather than in what you seek to accomplish.

When God opened my eyes, 1 John 5:3 made perfect sense: "For this is the love of God, that we keep his commandments. And his commandments are not burdensome." God's commands are no longer burdensome when you are living from your true spiritual birth. Since you know He loves you because He is love, you trust that His commands are for your good. Thus, you don't do them grudgingly, but willingly. I think this truth is echoed by Paul in Romans 5:1: "Therefore, since we have been justified by faith, we have peace with God through our Lord Jesus Christ." May your true birth bring you to an obedience to God that is no longer burdensome.

Questions:

1. Have you been prone to lean to a works-based theology? In what ways?

2. How can you continue to live obediently out of your spiritual birth through trust in Jesus Christ rather than putting confidence in the flesh?

3. List some ways you have found that His commandments are not burdensome.

Day Forty-Two

The Letters of John

God Produces Overcomers

Connected with Him in His love, I am more than conqueror;
without Him, I am nothing. Like some railway tickets in Ameri-
ca, I am "Not good if detached."
Corrie Ten Boom[1]

Text: 1 John 5:4-5
[4] For everyone who has been born of God overcomes the
world. And this is the victory that has overcome the world–our
faith. [5] Who is it that overcomes the world except the one who
believes that Jesus is the Son of God?

Thoughts:
Rod Mattoon, in *Treasures from First John*, introduces our
Scripture for today with these words:

> John focuses on the victory of the Christian. He refers
> to those who have been born again, who believe that Je-
> sus is the Son of God, as overcomers of this world. This
> word "overcomer" is from the Greek word *nikao* which
> means "to conquer, to be victorious; to defeat."
> This word *nikao* was popular with the Greek people.
> They worshiped a false goddess Nike who was considered
> the goddess of victory. In Greek mythology, she aided
> Zeus in his battle against the Titans.

Greeks believed that ultimate victory could not be achieved by mortal men, but only by the Greek gods and their help. John uses this word to show the victory that Christians have over this world and that victory comes through the Son of God, the Lord Jesus Christ. [2]

John writes, "…everyone who has been born of God overcomes the world." A supernatural birth results in a supernatural life.

If you are born of the Spirit, the Spirit gives you the supernatural ability to live the life of an overcomer. Therefore, your faith in God leads to His victory through your life. That is the reason John could write: "And this is the victory that has overcome the world–our faith."

If that wasn't clear enough, John added these words in verse 5: "Who is it that overcomes the world except the one who believes that Jesus is the Son of God?" Eugene Peterson, author of *The Message*, paraphrases 1 John 5:4-5 as follows:

[4-5]Every God-born person conquers the world's ways. The conquering power that brings the world to its knees is our faith. The person who wins out over the world's ways is simply the one who believes Jesus is the Son of God.

The *New Living Translation* words it this way:

[4] For every child of God defeats this evil world, and we achieve this victory through our faith.[5] And who can win this battle against the world? Only those who believe that Jesus is the Son of God.

The same power that provided the miraculous birth produces an extraordinary life. You could say it is only natural for the Holy Spirit to birth children who grow up to live supernaturally.

It is only fitting that we close today's devotion with words from John Yates's hymn, "Faith is the Victory."

> Encamped along the hills of light,
> Ye Christian soldiers, rise.
> And press the battle ere the night
> Shall veil the glowing skies.
> Against the foe in vales below
> Let all our strength be hurled.
> Faith is the victory, we know,
> That overcomes the world.
>
> His banner over us is love,
> Our sword the Word of God.
> We tread the road the saints above
> With shouts of triumph trod.
> By faith, they like a whirlwind's breath,
> Swept on o'er every field.
> The faith by which they conquered death
> Is still our shining shield.
>
> Faith is the victory! Faith is the victory!
> O glorious victory, that overcomes the world.[3]

Questions:

1. If you are a believer, do you reflect often on your new birth that led you into this new life? Why or why not? If you are not a believer, consider what your future faith would mean to your future victory.

2. How can you grow spiritually into all that you were supernaturally birthed to become?

3. Now that you know a little about John Yates's life, how can the message of "Faith is the Victory" impact your life?

4. It has been said, "The same faith that saves us sustains us." How can you live daily in light of that truth as an overcomer in Jesus Christ?

Day Forty-Three

The Letters of John

The Testimony of God Is Greater

This God—his way is perfect;
the word of the Lord proves true;
he is a shield for all those who take refuge in him.
Psalm 18:30

The heavens declare his righteousness,
for God himself is judge!
Psalm 50:6

Text: 1 John 5:6-9
⁶ This is he who came by water and blood—Jesus Christ; not by the water only but by the water and the blood. And the Spirit is the one who testifies, because the Spirit is the truth. ⁷ For there are three that testify: ⁸ the Spirit and the water and the blood; and these three agree. ⁹ If we receive the testimony of men, the testimony of God is greater, for this is the testimony of God that he has borne concerning his Son.

Thoughts:
   While there have been various interpretations of the meaning of the water, blood, and the Spirit, two things are clear from this passage of Scripture: all three (the Spirit, the water, and the blood) agree in their testimony concerning Jesus, and the testimony of God is greater than the testimony of men.

The need for multiple agreeing testimonies dates back to the Mosaic Law:

Deuteronomy 19:15 (ESV)
¹⁵ "A single witness shall not suffice against a person for any crime or for any wrong in connection with any offense that he has committed. Only on the evidence of two witnesses or of three witnesses shall a charge be established."

Thus, the emphasis on three witnesses found in the incarnation of Jesus Christ mentioned in 1 John 5:6-8 has roots dating back to the Torah. Three witnesses provided protection against false accusations. You could not be convicted if falsely accused by one malicious witness.

It is interesting to note that it was two false witnesses that gave false testimony against Jesus before His crucifixion:

Mark 14:55-59 (ESV)
⁵⁵ Now the chief priests and the whole council were seeking testimony against Jesus to put him to death, but they found none. ⁵⁶ For many bore false witness against him, but their testimony did not agree. ⁵⁷ And some stood up and bore false witness against him, saying, ⁵⁸ "We heard him say, 'I will destroy this temple that is made with hands, and in three days I will build another, not made with hands.'" ⁵⁹ Yet even about this their testimony did not agree.

During the trials against Jesus, the religious leaders couldn't find three people who could agree in their testimony against him for an obvious reason—our sinless Savior was an innocent lamb led to the slaughter (Isaiah 53:7). Jesus was falsely convicted by two witnesses who couldn't even get their stories straight.

But if three lying witnesses could get their testimony straight, an innocent man could be convicted. So, God's law contained a clause that challenged witnesses to tell the truth. A false witness in biblical times would receive the punishment due for the crime of which they falsely accused another:

Deuteronomy 19:16-19 (ESV)
[16] "If a malicious witness arises to accuse a person of wrongdoing, [17] then both parties to the dispute shall appear before the Lord, before the priests and the judges who are in office in those days. [18] The judges shall inquire diligently, and if the witness is a false witness and has accused his brother falsely, [19] then you shall do to him as he had meant to do to his brother. So you shall purge the evil from your midst."

We discover that a testimony was not validated simply by the number of witnesses. The one critical requirement was the character of the witness. The testimony of God is always greater than the testimony of men, because God's character is perfect. Remember what John declared about God's character in 1 John 1:5:

This is the message we have heard from him and proclaim to you, that God is light, and in him is no darkness at all.

Questions:

1. In a court of law, why is the number and character of the witnesses of extreme importance?

2. How does it strike you that Jesus was falsely accused by multiple witnesses who couldn't even get their stories to agree?

3. If we are willing to receive the testimony of men, how much more important is it that we receive the testimony of God?

4. Who all testified about Jesus at His baptism?

Matthew 3:16-17 (ESV)

[16] And when Jesus was baptized, immediately he went up from the water, and behold, the heavens were opened to him, and he saw the Spirit of God descending like a dove and coming to rest on him; [17] and behold, a voice from heaven said, "This is my beloved Son, with whom I am well pleased."

Day Forty-Four

The Letters of John

This Is the Testimony

This is God's essential message to man; that eternal life is a gift from God, received in Jesus Christ. It is all about Jesus, and living in Jesus is the evidence of eternal life.
David Guzik[1]

Text: 1 John 5:10-12
[10] Whoever believes in the Son of God has the testimony in himself. Whoever does not believe God has made him a liar, because he has not believed in the testimony that God has borne concerning his Son. [11] And this is the testimony, that God gave us eternal life, and this life is in his Son. [12] Whoever has the Son has life; whoever does not have the Son of God does not have life.

Thoughts:
Those who reject the testimony of the humanity and deity of Jesus Christ, are in essence, calling God a liar. God testifies that Jesus is the Son of God sent to save the world. When a person says otherwise, they speak directly against the testimony of God.

John declares that if we believe in the Son of God, we also have within us this testimony. The authors of the *Life Application Commentary* explain 1 John 5:10 with these words:

When people become God's children (by believing that Jesus is *the Son of God*), they know that salvation is sure because they *have the testimony in their hearts* – the testimony or witness of God himself (5:9). They know without any doubt because the Spirit who regenerated them gives them an inner witness to that reality (see Romans 8:16; Galatians 4:6). God's Spirit, alive in their spirit, witnesses to the fact that everything Jesus said and did was true. In fact, that is the primary function of the Spirit – to testify and reveal Jesus to every believer (see John 14:26; 15:26; 16:7–13).[2]

And what is this testimony? John emphatically states it in 1 John 5:11: ". . . God gave us eternal life, and this life is in his Son." David Allen, in *Preaching the Word* commentary, shares this insight:

> John turns to the jury and now begins his closing argument (vv. 11, 12). "The testimony of the witnesses is clear and irrefutable. God has given us eternal life, and this life is in his Son, Jesus. He who has the Son possesses this eternal life. He who does not have the Son of God does not have eternal life. As an old man, let me cut through the fog and speak with clear simplicity. Argue all you want, talk about all the gray areas you want, but the issue is clear-cut. I was there when Jesus died for our sins on that cross. I am a personal eyewitness, as I have already reminded you in 1 John 1:1–4. I was the first to see the empty tomb. I was there in the Upper Room a week after Jesus' resurrection when he appeared to his twelve disciples. I was there when Jesus ascended to Heaven. From that day until this, I have been telling others about this Jesus. I wrote

five books about it in your Bibles, telling you that Jesus is the Son of God. Whoever has the Son as his Savior possesses this eternal life. Whoever does not have this Son as his Savior does not have eternal life. If you don't have Jesus, you don't have life, but only death. If you die apart from Jesus, you will spend an eternity apart from Jesus in a place called Hell."[3]

Questions:

1. How is your belief in Jesus connected to your testimony about Him

2. Have you ever considered that those who reject Jesus are calling God a liar? What are your thoughts on this truth?

3. How does today's Scripture passage challenge you to live out your testimony for Jesus?

Day Forty-Five

The Letters of John

The Purpose Statement of John's Letter

John wants no one to be left behind.
He wants every reader to have Christ and have eternal
life. And He wants us to live with total confidence about the
security of that relationship and the certainty of where we
stand "in the Lord." This is the way to live.
David Case and David Holdren[1]

Text: 1 John 5:13
[13] I write these things to you who believe in the name of the
Son of God, that you may know that you have eternal life.

Thoughts:
It is believed that John wrote the Gospel of John, the three
letters of John, and the book of Revelation. In each of these
three works, John clearly states his purpose for writing. These
purposes are keys that unlock the truths of each writing.

In the Gospel of John, he allows you to almost get through
reading the book, and then he gives you the key.

John 20:31 (ESV)
[31] but these are written so that you may believe that Jesus is
the Christ, the Son of God, and that by believing you may have
life in his name.

The Gospel of John was written that we might believe that Jesus is the Son of God.

In the Letters of John, it is found in our verse of study for today.

1 John 5:13 (ESV)
[13] I write these things to you who believe in the name of the Son of God, that you may know that you have eternal life.

In the Gospel, John wants you to believe; in his letters, you need assurance. What you believe about Jesus leads to assurance about what you know.

Daniel Akin's words from *Exalting Jesus in 1,2,3 John* help us focus on the meaning of 1 John 5:13:

> The apostle John tells us it is possible to have eternal life, the very life of God, and yet have doubts. However, he does not want us to have doubts. He wants us to have assurance. Therefore, he provides multiple tests throughout the book ("these things" in verse 13 refers specifically to 5:1–12, but in general, the phrase refers to the entire book), revolving around the three themes of belief, obedience, and love. Those who believe Jesus is the Son of God, pursue obedience, and love others can be assured they have eternal life right now. Today! [2]

Lehman Strauss brings us to an even deeper understanding of today's verse:

> The Gospel according to John was written that we might believe in Jesus Christ and be saved. The purpose of the Epistle is not merely that we might possess eternal life through believing, but that we may know

that we possess it. The word *know* in 1 John 5:13 is the Greek word *oida*. There is a difference between *ginosko* and *oida*. *Ginosko* suggests progress in knowledge; *oida* suggests fullness of knowledge, or to know perfectly, beyond the possibility of a doubt. Saving faith in Jesus Christ gives the believer assurance that can never be destroyed.

Seven times in chapter 5 we find the assuring words, "we know." The Christian possesses a knowing faith because Christianity is a religion of certainties. The child of God can be certain about his *past sins* (2 Timothy 1:12), his *present sufficiency* (Romans 8:28), and his *prospective security* (2 Corinthians 5:1). This is having a knowing faith, and it grows out of a saving faith. Without faith in Christ, we cannot possess His life. Without knowing that we have that life, we cannot enjoy and live it to the full. We need to know with a knowledge that is final and certain that we have eternal life.[3]

Questions:

1. Why is it essential that a believer walks with a full assurance of his or her salvation?

2. In what ways do you see the enemy attacking people in the area of the security of their salvation?

3. In what ways do you see a connection between John's purpose statements found in his Gospel and his Letter?

Day Forty-Six

The Letters of John

Praying According to His Will

Prayer is a mighty instrument,
not for getting man's will done in Heaven,
but for getting God's will done on earth.
Robert Law [1]

Prayer is not overcoming God's reluctance.
It is laying hold of God's willingness.
George Mueller [2]

Text: 1 John 5:14-15

[14] And this is the confidence that we have toward him, that if we ask anything according to his will he hears us. [15] And if we know that he hears us in whatever we ask, we know that we have the requests that we have asked of him.

Thoughts:

1 John 5:14-15, if not taken in context, can lead to a dangerous misinterpretation of Scripture. Some false teachers have taken these verses to mean that God will do whatever you ask for in prayer. This is a grievous misunderstanding and misrepresentation of John's teaching here.

These two verses are intricately connected to the surrounding verses and to John's other teachings on prayer. The "and" to begin verse 14 connects back to verse 13 where John states,

"I write these things to you who believe in the name of the Son of God, that you may know that you have eternal life." Just as believers can know they have eternal life; they can know that God answers prayers.

Brian Harbour reveals how 1 John 5:14-15 relates to John's other writings on the requirements of prayer:

> We find some conditions for answered prayer in the Johannine writings:
> - We must ask in his name, according to John 14:14.
> - We must abide in him and his words must abide in us, according to John 15:7.
> - We must keep his commandments, according to 1 John 3:22.
> - And, in our text for today, we must ask in accordance with his will.
>
> Within those given conditions, we know that God answers prayer. When God's children open their lives to God in prayer, God hears and answers those prayers.[3]

So, the key words in 1 John 5:14-15 are, "if we ask anything according to his will." David Guzik expounds on these words:

> God would have us ask according to His will. It is easy for us to only be concerned with *our* will before God, and to have a fatalistic view regarding His will ("He will accomplish His will with or without my prayers anyway, won't He?"). But God wants us to see and discern His will through His Word, and to pray His will into action. When John wrote this, John may have had Jesus' own words in mind, which he recorded in John 15:7: *If you abide in Me, and My words abide in you, you will ask what you desire, and it shall be done for you.* When we *abide* in Jesus

– living in Him, day by day – then our will becomes more and more aligned with His will, and we can *ask what you desire*, and more and more be asking according to His will. Then we see answered prayer.[4]

John writes these words in the last half of verse 15: "we know that we have the requests that we have asked of him." Warren Wiersbe gives profound insight into this statement:

John does not write, "We *shall have* the requests," but, "We *know* that we have the requests" (1 John 5:15). The verb is present tense. We may not see the answer to a prayer immediately, but we have inner confidence that God has answered.[5]

Questions:

1. Have you seen these verses taken out of context? In what ways?

2. Why is your abiding in Christ so foundational to praying in His will?

3. How can these verses give you confidence that God does indeed answer prayer? How can 1 John 5:14-15 strengthen your desire to draw closer to Him?

Day Forty-Seven

The Letters of John

The Seriousness of Sin

A man that knows that he lives in sin against God
will not be inclined to come daily into the presence of God.
Jonathan Edwards [1]

Text: 1 John 5:16-19

[16] If anyone sees his brother committing a sin not leading to death, he shall ask, and God will give him life–to those who commit sins that do not lead to death. There is sin that leads to death; I do not say that one should pray for that. [17] All wrongdoing is sin, but there is sin that does not lead to death. [18] We know that everyone who has been born of God does not keep on sinning, but he who was born of God protects him, and the evil one does not touch him. [19] We know that we are from God, and the whole world lies in the power of the evil one.

Thoughts:

This is one of the most difficult passages in the Bible to explain. Even Greek scholar Kenneth Wuest confessed his utter inability to understand "the sin that leads to death."

In *A Commentary in the Wesleyan Tradition*, Rick Williamson explains this difficult passage as follows:

> The sin that leads to death for John referred to sins
> that were incompatible with being children of God. These

174

sins would include denying that Jesus is the Christ, the Son of God (2:22–23); refusing to obey God's commands (2:4); loving the world (2:15–17); and hating fellow believers (2:9, 11; 3:15; 4:20).[2]

While some of today's Scripture is perplexing, one thing is profoundly clear: Sin is serious. John divides the sins that a Christian commits into two categories. There are sins that lead to death and sins that do not lead to death. This does not mean that some sins are serious, and some are not. John quickly adds the words, "All wrongdoing is sin."

After dealing with this short discussion on sin, John shifts his emphasis towards the victory every believer has over sin. Our new life in Christ does not lead to a pattern or lifestyle of sin. This is the same point John made back in chapter 3 of 1 John.

1 John 3:9 (NLT)

[9] Those who have been born into God's family do not make a practice of sinning, because God's life is in them. So they can't keep on sinning, because they are children of God.

God protects His children and will not allow the devil to touch His own. Sin and its consequences are to be taken seriously, but in Christ, each child of God is given supernatural power to overcome sin and to obey the will of God.

In 1 John 5:19, John gives another statement that begins with "we know." Daniel Akin, in the *New American Commentary*, explains this verse as follows:

What was expressed in vs. 18 is now enunciated in terms of a general principle in vs. 19. "We know that we are the children of God, and that the whole world is under the control of the evil one." This is the second "we know" of vs. 18–20. God's people are comforted with the certainty that God is their Father and that he will protect them. The second half of the assertion is that "the whole world is under control of the evil one." The evil one does not touch the Christian, but the world is helplessly in its grasp. There are only two possible positions. Everyone is either "of God" or "under the control of the evil one." Neutrality is not possible.[4]

Questions:

1. How do you feel about the fact that there is a sin that leads to death?

2. Are you prone to rationalize, justify, and make excuses for the sin in your life? In what ways can today's Scripture give you a more serious approach to dealing with sin in your life?

3. When you are tempted to sin, why is it important for you to know that God protects His children? In what ways are you living under His protection?

4. How does 1 John 3:4 relate to today's Scripture?

1 John 3:4 (ESV)
⁴ Everyone who makes a practice of sinning also practices lawlessness; sin is lawlessness.

Day Forty-Eight

The Letters of John

We Know the Truth

Truth always carries with it confrontation. Truth demands
confrontation, loving confrontation, nevertheless.
If our reflex action is always accommodation regardless of
the centrality of truth involved, there is something wrong.
Francis Shaeffer [1]

Text: 1 John 5:20
[20] And we know that the Son of God has come and has given us
understanding, so that we may know him who is true; and we
are in him who is true, in his Son Jesus Christ. He is the true God
and eternal life.

Thoughts:
    The apostle John had a deep love for the truth that is obvi-
ous in his writings. For John, there were no gray areas. He didn't
mince words. He sets light against darkness, life against death,
obedience against disobedience, love against hatred, and truth
against lies.
    It doesn't take long for Jesus to change someone's life. In an
instant, the light of Jesus drives away the darkness. If God can
do all that in a second, just think what could happen over three
years. That's how long John walked with Christ. In that time period, Jesus changed the son of thunder into an apostle of love!
John was a man that walked in the balance of truth and love.

John's love for the truth is evidenced in his writing. John uses the Greek word for truth, *aletheia*, twenty-five times in the book of John and twenty times in his letters. No one except Jesus had more to say in Scripture about truth.

It makes perfect sense, then, for John to get to the end of his first letter and write about the truth. 1 John 5:20 is full of John's conviction about the truth. Note how many times he uses the word in just the last half of verse 20: ". . . we may know him who is true; and we are in him who is true, in his Son Jesus Christ. He is the true God and eternal life."

David Allen, in *Preaching the Word* commentary, says:

> In this context truth's primary meaning is that which is real, not illusory. It has substance, permanence, and reality. In a world full of people longing for the real thing but grasping at illusions, John offers the truth: Jesus Christ and his gospel. It is as if John is saying, "This God of whom I have been affirming that Jesus Christ is his sole Revealer, and of whom I have been declaring that through him we may know God and dwell abidingly in him, this—and no one else—is the true God." "We ... know him who is true [real]." "We are in him who is true." This is eternal life. John began this letter in 1:2, 3 talking about eternal life, and now he concludes where he began. What is eternal life? It is knowing him who is true and being in him who is true. That is eternal life: knowing God and being in Christ. And John says we better know that we know! "I have no confidence in my confidence. I place no reliance upon my own assurance. My assurance lies in the fact that 'Christ Jesus came into the world to save sinners,' and that 'Whosoever believeth in Him hath everlasting life.' I do believe in Him, and therefore I know I have eternal life."[2]

Questions:

1. In what ways does the world seek to destroy the truth? Are you prone to watering down the truth? In what ways?

2. John, the one whom Jesus loved, spoke more about the truth than anyone except Jesus. Why is it essential to have both truth and love?

3. How is John's description of Jesus in the Gospel of John connected to his belief in 1 John 5:20 that, "He is the true God and eternal life."

John 1:14 (ESV)

¹⁴ And the Word became flesh and dwelt among us, and we have seen his glory, glory as of the only Son from the Father, full of grace and truth.

Day Forty-Nine

The Letters of John

Warning Against Idolatry

If you love anything more than God, you are an idolater.
If there is anything you would not
give up for God, it is your idol.
If there is anything that you seek with greater fervor
than you seek the glory of God, that is your idol.
Conversion means turning from every idol.
Charles Spurgeon[1]

Text: 1 John 5:21

[21] Little children, keep yourselves from idols.

Thoughts:

David Guzik gives incredible discernment into John's last statement of 1 John:

> This may seem like a strange way to end John's letter, but it fits in with the theme of a real, living relationship with God. The enemy to fellowship with God is idolatry: embracing a false god, or a false idea of the true God. John rightly closes with this warning, after having spent much of the book warning us against the dangers of the false Jesus many were teaching in his day (1 John 3:18–23; 4:1–3; 5:6–9).

We can only have a *real relationship* with the God who is *really there!* Idolatry, whether obvious (praying to a statue) or subtle (living for your career or someone other than God) will always choke out a *real relationship* with God and damage our relationships with our brothers and sisters in Christ. No wonder John ends with keep yourselves from idols; this is how we protect our relationship with God.[2]

Those who have been born of God have a knowledge of the one true God. A true knowledge of God leads to a life of light and love. Worship of idols is completely inconsistent and incompatible with a real relationship with the one true God.

Warren Wiersbe's words on this warning against idolatry are extremely insightful. Wiersbe also connects 1 John 5:21 to the Gospel of John:

This is the secret of the life that is real. Because we have met the true God, through His Son Jesus Christ, we are in contact with reality. Our fellowship is with a God who is genuine. As we have seen, the word "real" means "the original as opposed to a copy" and "the authentic as opposed to an imitation." Jesus Christ is the true Light (John 1:9), and true Bread (John 6:32), and true Vine (John 15:1), and Truth itself (John 14:6). He is the Original; everything else is a copy. He is authentic; everything else is only an imitation.

Christians live in an atmosphere of reality. Most unsaved people live in an atmosphere of pretense and sham. Christians have been given spiritual discernment to know the true from the false, but the unsaved do not have this understanding. Christians do not simply choose between good and bad; they choose between true and false. An idol represents that which is false and empty; and a person who lives for idols will himself become false and empty.

Few people today bow to idols of wood and metal. Nevertheless, other idols capture their attention and affection. *Covetousness*, for example, is idolatry (Col. 3:5). A man may worship his bankbook or his stock portfolio just as fervently as a so-called heathen worships his ugly idol. "Thou shalt worship the Lord thy God, and Him only shalt thou serve" (Matt. 4:10). *The thing we serve is the thing we worship!* Whatever controls our lives and "calls the signals" is our god.

This explains why God warns us against the sin of idolatry. Not only is it a violation of His commandment (Ex. 20:1–6), but it is a subtle way for Satan to take control of us. When "things" take God's place in our lives, we are guilty of idolatry. This means we are living for the *un*real instead of for the *real*.

A Christian has "turned to God from idols to serve the living and true God" (1 Thessalonians 1:9). Idols are dead, but Christ is the living God. Idols are false, but Christ is the true God. This is the secret of the life that is real!

So John's admonition, "Keep yourselves from idols," can be paraphrased, "Watch out for the imitation and the artificial and be real!"[3]

Questions:

1. Why is it significant that John closes his first letter with a warning against idolatry?

2. Read the first two commandments God gave Moses. Why does God both command and warn against idolatry?

Exodus 20:3-6 (ESV)

³ "You shall have no other gods before me. ⁴ You shall not make for yourself a carved image, or any likeness of anything that is in heaven above, or that is in the earth beneath, or that is in the water under the earth. ⁵ You shall not bow down to them or serve them, for I the Lord your God am a jealous God, visiting the iniquity of the fathers on the children to the third and the fourth generation of those who hate me, ⁶ but showing stead-fast love to thousands of those who love me and keep my com-mandments."

3. Examine your heart and write down your current priorities in life. What or who are you the most passionate about? Are you guilty of idolatry in any areas of your life?

Day Fifty

The Letters of John

Grace, Mercy, and Peace

God's grace is immeasurable, His mercy is inexhaustible,
and His peace is inexpressible.
Anonymous

Text: 2 John 1:1-3
¹ The elder to the elect lady and her children, whom I love in truth, and not only I, but also all who know the truth, ² because of the truth that abides in us and will be with us forever: ³ Grace, mercy, and peace will be with us, from God the Father and from Jesus Christ the Father's Son, in truth and love.

Thoughts:
John wrote the short letter of 2 John "to the elect lady and her children." Most commentators interpret this language as a description of a local church and its members:

John probably wrote the short letter of 2 John to a local church as a brief follow-up to his first letter. He repeats many of the same ideas and addresses some of the same problems. Apparently, the false teachers were traveling around, trying to come into the churches under the guise of godly teachers who could take you farther in your Christian faith (2 John 9). But they denied essential truth about Jesus Christ. So John writes this short letter before he could make a personal visit, to warn the church about not receiving these men into their midst. In doing so, he gives us a prescription for a healthy church.

There are two parts: First, for the church to be healthy, she must be sensitive to the life within (1–6). Second, she must be on guard to the dangers without (7–13).[1]

John opens his second letter with a threefold greeting (vs. 3): "Grace, mercy, and peace." The following explanation of John's greeting comes from a combination of two commentaries on 2 John: *The Life Application Commentary* and the *Steven J. Cole Commentary Series*. May their words provide both clear explanation and practical application of John's greeting in his second letter:

> "Grace" means God's undeserved favor shown to sinners whereby he saves them and gives them strength to live for him. The only other time John wrote of grace was in John 1:16–17: "From the fullness of his grace we have all received one blessing after another. For the law was given through Moses; grace and truth came through Jesus Christ." The Greek text of John 1:16 indicates that God gives grace to believers as a continual supply.
>
> God reveals his "mercy" by forgiving and freeing people from sin, resulting in peace between them and God.
>
> "Peace" refers to the peace that Christ made between sinners and God through his death on the cross. Peace also refers to that inner assurance and tranquility that God places in the heart, producing confidence and contentment in Christ.
>
> Grace, mercy, and peace keep on coming like a spring-fed well that never runs dry. Grace *from God the Father and from Jesus Christ* can never be exhausted;

God always makes it available to believers.

The title *God the Father* points to the unique relationship Christians have with God. He is a father to them; they are his children. Jesus Christ, referred to here as *the Father's Son,* points to the unique relationship between God and Jesus. While all believers can call God their Father, only Jesus is the unique Son of God who is one with God himself.

Truth and love form a bridge into the remainder of the letter. John speaks more directly about truth in verses 2 and 4 and about love in verse 5. Truth and love always go hand in hand.[2] "In truth and love" probably means that these blessings are experienced by those who continue to hold to the truth and practice love for one another.[2]

John's salutation varies from the usual form of a prayer, "Grace, mercy, and peace be with you." Rather, John emphatically (in the Greek text) states, "Grace, mercy, and peace *will be* with *us.*" Then, after "from God the Father and from Jesus Christ," he adds, "the Son of the Father, in truth and love."

The application of John's opening greeting is that being a part of a local church is not primarily a matter of attending services or joining the church, as important as those things are. Rather, it is a matter of coming into a personal relationship with God through His Son, Jesus Christ. To be a part of His church means that you have personally experienced His grace, mercy, and peace through His salvation. And it means that you hold firmly to the truth about Jesus Christ.[3]

Questions:

1. How would you define each part of John's threefold greeting: Grace, mercy, and peace?

2. How important is the order of this threefold greeting?

3. How is God's grace, mercy, and peace applied "in truth and love"?

4. What thoughts come to your mind when you think about the fact that God's grace, mercy, and peace will be with you (future tense)?

Day Fifty-One

The Letters of John

Our Walk Is Our Witness

For to this you have been called,
because Christ also suffered for you,
leaving you an example,
so that you might follow in his steps.
1 Peter 2:21

Therefore, as you received Christ Jesus
the Lord, so walk in him . . .
Colossians 2:6

Text: 2 John 1:4-11

⁴ I rejoiced greatly to find some of your children walking in the truth, just as we were commanded by the Father. ⁵ And now I ask you, dear lady—not as though I were writing you a new commandment, but the one we have had from the beginning—that we love one another. ⁶ And this is love, that we walk according to his commandments; this is the commandment, just as you have heard from the beginning, so that you should walk in it. ⁷ For many deceivers have gone out into the world, those who do not confess the coming of Jesus Christ in the flesh. Such a one is the deceiver and the antichrist. ⁸ Watch yourselves, so that you may not lose what we have worked for, but may win a full reward. ⁹ Everyone who goes on ahead and does not abide in the teaching of Christ, does not have God. Whoever abides

in the teaching has both the Father and the Son. **¹⁰** If anyone comes to you and does not bring this teaching, do not receive him into your house or give him any greeting, **¹¹** for whoever greets him takes part in his wicked works.

Thoughts:

John begins the main portion of his second letter with rejoicing. Like a father watching his children grow up, the apostle John celebrated with those who were growing closer to Christ.

It's always encouraging when you see children walking in the faith in which they were raised. I've always appreciated hearing the good news about someone's son, daughter, or grandchild I hadn't heard about for years – that he or she has maintained a Christian walk, or is involved in church ministry or missions, or is passing the faith on to their own children. It doesn't always work that way, and there's no guarantee that all of our children will faithfully walk in the truth.

The apostle John puts it a little more realistically. He says that "some" of her children were walking in the truth. The way the Greek reads, the "some" who were faithful to their spiritual roots could refer to a majority or to a minority. The fact that John is overjoyed at what he had learned, though, suggests that the faithfulness of the children was the rule rather than the exception. Still, not all of them were faithful.

This highlights an important principle of spiritual nurturing and discipleship. Both our physical families and our spiritual families will have members who deviate from the teaching of parents or mentors. I've experienced this firsthand and have seen it in countless families throughout my ministry. It breaks our hearts when it happens. It drives us to prayer in the hopes that those children will one day return. However, when some go astray, we shouldn't lose sight of those who remain on the "truth walk." John didn't dwell on those who had taken a spiritual detour but on those who had received the commandment to walk in the truth (1:4).

What does this "walking in truth" look like? To define this, John refers to Christ's original command that we "love one another" (1:5; see John 13:34). This isn't a new command, but one that had characterized the Christian life from the beginning. Loving one another and walking in truth were not meant to be an either-or prospect. If we love someone unconditionally, but they are distracting us from the truth, then we may need to infuse more truth into the relationship. John goes on to say, "This is love, that we walk according to His commandments" (2 John 1:6).

It doesn't have to be one or the other – either standing strong in the truth or showing love toward others. In actuality, the test of true love is whether it leads us closer to Christ. It never compromises Christ's standards for the sake of a loosely defined unity. It never consents to sin in the name of grace and tolerance. This point bears repeating: Unconditional love must be balanced by discerning truth.[1]

John has continually connected our Christian walk to our witness for Christ. In 1 John 1:7, he calls us to walk in the light. In 1 John 2:6, John states that "whoever says he abides in him ought to walk in the same way in which he walked." In 1 John 2:11, he reminds us that whoever hates his brother "walks in the darkness." 1 John 3:11-18 and 1 John 4:7-21 give a detailed discussion of walking in love. John begins 1 John 5 emphasizing the overcoming nature of our walk with the Lord.

Here in 2 John, he adds two more descriptions to the believer's walk. In 2 John 1:4, he rejoices that some are walking in the truth. In 2 John 1:6, John writes that true love is walking "according to his commandments." Therefore, believers walk in the truth and in obedience as they walk in love.

Because our walk is our witness, our walk is extremely important. Therefore, in 2 John 1:7-11, John cautions believers about false teachers who deceive people in their walk with the Lord. Notice how John includes himself in his words of warning: "Watch yourselves, so that you may not lose what we have worked for, but may win a full reward." John counsels God's children not to compromise our walk because it will harm our witness.

Questions:

1. How is your walk with Christ in the following areas?

    Walking in Light

    Walking in Love

    Walking in Truth

    Walking in Obedience

2. Are there any areas of your walk that don't match your witness?

3. Someone once said, "Tell me who you hang out with, and I will tell you who you are." Along with today's Scripture, how do the following verses relate to this saying?

Psalm 1:1-2 (ESV)
   [1] Blessed is the man who walks not in the counsel of the wicked, nor stands in the way of sinners, nor sits in the seat of scoffers; [2] but his delight is in the law of the Lord, and on his law he meditates day and night.

Proverbs 13:20 (ESV)
   [20] Whoever walks with the wise becomes wise, but the companion of fools will suffer harm.

1 Corinthians 15:33 (ESV)
   [33] Do not be deceived: "Bad company ruins good morals."

Day Fifty-Two

The Letters of John

The Joy of Face-to-Face Fellowship

Our relationship with God will never be right
as long as our relationship with others is wrong.
Allistair Begg[1]

Beware of anything that separates us from godly people.
Beth Moore[2]

Text: 2 John 1:12-13
[12] Though I have much to write to you, I would rather not use paper and ink. Instead I hope to come to you and talk face to face, so that our joy may be complete. [13] The children of your elect sister greet you.

Thoughts:
A personal relationship with Jesus Christ leads to genuine relationships with others in our family of faith. Our joy in Jesus leads to joyful fellowship with others. Charles Swindoll explains John's emphasis as he closes out his second letter:

John ends this tiny letter with some personal greetings. The warmth of his affection comes through as he expresses his earnest desire to see God's children "face to face." He had so much more to say, but paper and ink weren't the proper medium. What a great endorsement of the need for personal, in-the-flesh, life-on-life interaction! Even in his old age, John wanted to make the trip to be present with his brothers and sisters in Christ. This is a lesson all of us could learn in our impersonal world of texting, e-mail, and social media. Personal presence matters. Only through face-to-face interaction would John be able to make their joy full and complete (1:12).[3]

Many people today live in isolation. We can shop for anything we need without ever leaving our house. If we do have to leave our house, we can have our order delivered to our car without ever going into the store. Many people live in gated communities, with fenced in backyards. We can drive into our enclosed carports and let the garage door down so that we never have to speak to our neighbors. Many of us have a camera and a speaker on our doorbell so we can look at someone at our door and speak to them without ever having to meet them personally.

And this social separation has found its way into the church. True relationships with believers have been exchanged for a façade of fellowship. In many ways, technology has replaced the personal. We text instead of talk. We email instead of experiencing true relational interaction. We have Zoom meetings instead of actually meeting together. Our impersonal world has led to major setbacks in our personal walk with God and others.

As far as it depends on you, let's get back to face-to-face encounters with our family of faith. We need to actually see each other, hug each other, and relate to one another so that we can grow to genuinely love one another. Let's turn our "hope to see you soon" into "come on in and sit down" so that our "joy may be complete."

Questions:

1. In the last few years, how has your life become more isolated?

2. In what ways have you seen social isolation negatively impact your church?

3. How can you take tangible steps to put the personal back into personal relationships with your family of faith?

Day Fifty-Three

The Letters of John

No Greater Joy

Greater joy is the outcome of children who walk in the truth. Parents are joyful; grandparents are joyful; mentors are joyful. The children are joyful. So, children walking in truth is an excellent goal for parents. Walk in the truth yourself, while at the same time training your children to do the same. Truth-walking is joyful living.
Boyd Bailey[1]

Text: 3 John 1:1-4
[1] The elder to the beloved Gaius, whom I love in truth. [2] Beloved, I pray that all may go well with you and that you may be in good health, as it goes well with your soul. [3] For I rejoiced greatly when the brothers came and testified to your truth, as indeed you are walking in the truth. [4] I have no greater joy than to hear that my children are walking in the truth.

Thoughts:
We begin John's third letter in our devotional today. 3 John is the shortest book in the Bible. When you read those words, you might think, "2 John has 13 verses and 3 John has 15 verses. So, 2 John is the shortest book." Yet, 2 John has 245 Greek words, and 3 John only has 219 words in the original language. This fact makes 3 John the shortest book in

all of Scripture. And as we will see today, the shortest book speaks about the greatest joy.

3 John is written to "the beloved Gaius" whom John truly loved. In verse 2, John prayed for everything to go well with Gaius physically and spiritually. He prayed for a healthy body and a nourished soul. In our society, many people focus on one to the exclusion of the other. Some people spend hours a day exercising their physical body, eating right, and living for a healthy heart. Yet these same people may spend five minutes working on their spiritual lives.

The reverse is also true. There are people who spend hours in the Word but fall to the sin of gluttony and do not take care of the physical temple that houses the Holy Spirit of God. In 3 John, John prays for a balance of growth in both areas of Gaius' life. A healthy soul and a body make a powerful combination as we seek to live closer to Christ.

In the verses that follow, John describes his joy for his beloved friend. The *Life Application Bible Commentary* and *Preaching the Word* Commentary give the following explanation of 3 John 1:3-4:

> In verses 3 and 4, John "rejoiced greatly" that his dear friend Gaius was faithful to the truth and living out the truth. John's faithful ministry had given birth to many spiritual children. Some of these no doubt came to faith in Christ through John's direct ministry. Since John was an apostle, all were in some way under his spiritual leadership. Like an old professor who learns that his former students have now distinguished themselves in their respective disciplines, nothing provides John any greater joy than to hear reports that "my children are walking in the truth."[2]

To "walk in the truth" means living out the truth by expressing it in one's behavior. Gaius was doing this, and John had *no greater joy* than to see it happen in the life of one of his spiritual children.[3]

Joy is the fruit in the life of every believer as they walk in the truth of God's Word. Joy is the glorious result of godly growth. When you love God with all your heart, mind, soul, and strength – the closer you get to Him in your personal relationship, the more elated you become. God's passions become your loves. Since God is passionate about others, you begin to truly love other people with a Christlike love. The more you love others in the truth, the greater your excitement becomes to see them grow in their personal relationship with God. As this progression happens in your life, a deep residing joy occurs when you witness those you love experiencing more of the transforming power of Jesus.

John said that he had no greater joy than to hear that the people he loved were walking in the truth. John, in the later years of his life, was still experiencing the joy of Jesus. Our greatest joy will always be experienced when we see those we love most grow in their walk with the One who loves them more than we do. There is no greater joy!

Questions:

1. What does 1 Corinthians 6:19-20 say about the importance of your physical health?

2. What do Jesus' words in Mathew 4:4 say about the significance of your spiritual health?

3. In what ways do you experience joy as you watch your children or those you mentor grow in the truth of God's Word?

Day Fifty-Four

The Letters of John

Fellow Workers for the Truth

The possessors of the truth are to be workers with the truth.
Alexander MacLaren[1]

Text: 3 John 1:5-8
[5] Beloved, it is a faithful thing you do in all your efforts for these brothers, strangers as they are, [6] who testified to your love before the church. You will do well to send them on their journey in a manner worthy of God. [7] For they have gone out for the sake of the name, accepting nothing from the Gentiles. [8] Therefore we ought to support people like these, that we may be fellow workers for the truth.

Thoughts:
Several scholars have referred to the small book of 3 John as the most personal book in the New Testament. Their reason for this description comes through the personal names John mentions in his third letter. You will notice three men John mentions by name: Gaius (vs. 1), Diotrephes (vs. 9), and Demetrius (vs. 12). While we don't know them personally, John does. And through John's narrative, we realize we know people just like them.

The first person John describes is Gaius. We gather from John's words that Gaius was a faithful worker in the local church. John wrote, ". . . it is a faithful thing you do in all your efforts for these brothers . . . who testified to your love for the church." Gaius was a hard worker who gave great efforts on behalf of other people in the church. He served selflessly so that other believers could grow in their walk with the Lord. Other people noticed his faithfulness and testified publicly about his Christian love.

We need more people like Gaius in our churches today. Often times, people come to church only for what they can get out of it. Their main focus is on themselves. When they complain, they make statements like, "I didn't get anything out of the service today" or "I left that church because I didn't get anything out of going." Perhaps they would have gotten more out of church if they had given more to it. They missed out on their blessing because they did not seek to be a blessing to others.

John comes to a significant conclusion in verse 8. He says, "Therefore we ought to support people like these, that we may be fellow workers for the truth." When we support other people who spread the name of Jesus, we become fellow workers for the truth. Not everyone can go to another city or country and share Jesus. However, those who cannot go can still support those that can. We can pray daily for missionaries, financially support them, host them in our homes, and find ways to encourage them. Every time we support them in any way, we join them as fellow workers for the truth.

May the following illustration from God's creation encourage you as you seek to be fellow workers for the truth:

> Huge redwood trees in California are considered the largest things on earth and the tallest trees in the world. Some of them are three hundred feet high and over 2,500 years old. One would think that trees so large would have a tremendous root system reaching down hundreds of feet into the earth. The redwoods actually

have a very shallow system of roots, but they all inter-
twine. They are locked to each other. When the storms
come or the winds blow, the redwoods stand. They are
locked to each other, and they don't stand alone, for all
the trees support and protect each other.[2]

Questions:

1. How can you support and protect other believers for the sake
of the name of Jesus Christ?

2. Who in your local church reminds you of Gaius? How are they
a special servant in your church?

3. Why is the unity of God's people essential in our labor for
Christ? How do your love and labor interlock for His glory? How
does your selflessness connect with your service to bring honor
to His name?

Day Fifty-Five

The Letters of John

The Diotrephes Disease

Pride: There is no fault which makes a man more unpopular,
and no fault which we are more unconscious of in ourselves.
And the more we have it ourselves,
the more we dislike it in others.
C.S. Lewis[1]

Text: 3 John 1:9-12
[9] I have written something to the church, but Diotrephes, who likes to put himself first, does not acknowledge our authority. [10] So if I come, I will bring up what he is doing, talking wicked nonsense against us. And not content with that, he refuses to welcome the brothers, and also stops those who want to and puts them out of the church. [11] Beloved, do not imitate evil but imitate good. Whoever does good is from God; whoever does evil has not seen God. [12] Demetrius has received a good testimony from everyone, and from the truth itself. We also add our testimony, and you know that our testimony is true.

Thoughts:
In today's text, we find two more men mentioned by name: Diotrephes and Demetrius. The first had caused trouble in the church. The second had received a good testimony from everyone. In today's devotion we will focus on the danger of Diotrephes.

David Case and David W. Holdren, in *A Commentary for Bible Students*, explain the problems John and the church had with Diotrephes:

He was a serious irritation to John and apparently many in the local congregation. John says that he wrote to the church (vs. 9) apparently the one where Gaius, Diotrephes, and others were involved together. Again, we do not know if this man had any official position in the church or was simply a layperson agitated over the hospitality issue. However, John gives us a clearer picture of what he was like.

Diotrephes loved to be first. Other translations use terms like "being in charge," "in control," or "being leader." In every group, there are those who are comfortable to lead if needed, those who are glad to follow, those who refuse to follow, and those who lead without being asked. Diotrephes qualified for two of those statements.

Diotrephes rejected established church leadership. John says that the man not only **loves to be first,** but he also **will have nothing to do with us.** He was overtly resisting the established leadership of the elder, John. It is unclear whether or not the whole congregation was under the thumb of Diotrephes, but at least he refused to recognize the appeals of John regarding the hospitality issue.

Diotrephes was engaged in malicious gossip. John says that if and when he came he would **call attention to what he is doing, gossiping maliciously about us** (vs. 10). The Greek words for this gossip have the meaning of "babbling incoherently or verbally fluent, but empty." This must have frustrated John, as it does any of us when we become aware that others are talking about us in ways that are demeaning, distorted, and disgraceful.

Diotrephes refused to welcome the guest missionaries. What more can be said, but that the man loved his local power base and was not about to yield it to anyone? It is even possible that this man was the ruling deacon of the congregation. Whoever he was, he alienated anyone who threatened his place of dominance among the people. In congregations like this, they rarely grow beyond a few dozen people because even outsiders can figure out the church politics fairly quickly, so they run for the next church or simply stay home."[2]

Charles Swindoll gives these wise words of application concerning people like Diotrephes:

I'd love to be able to say the days of Diotrephes are over, that they died in the first century, and that his spirit never made it out of those two verses in 3 John. Sadly, the spirit of Diotrephes outlived that era and continues into our own day

In my life of ministry, I can attest to the fact that an acute case of "Diotrephes Disease," with those kinds of symptoms, can bring an otherwise healthy church to its deathbed. As strong-minded but spiritually immature people weasel their way into positions of influence, they begin intimidating others to get their way. The problem usually isn't a matter of bad theology, but pride; not false teaching, but faulty leading. If left untreated, "Diotrephes Disease" can infect a whole congregation, leading to conflict, schism, and the death of a local church.

The apostle John also knew exactly where that original outbreak of "Diotrephes Disease" would end if it didn't get isolated and removed. This is why he mentions in 1:10, "If I come, I will call attention to his deeds."[3]

We need to eliminate the "Diotrephes Disease" from our churches. In addition, we need more people with a good reputation like Demetrius.

Questions:

1. In what ways have you witnessed the "Diotrephes Disease" in your local church?

2. Why is it important that people like Diotrephes are quickly confronted with truth and in love?

3. How are John's words in 3 John 1:11 incredibly valuable in dealing with others in the local church?

> [11] Beloved, do not imitate evil but imitate good. Whoever does good is from God; whoever does evil has not seen God.

4. There is not much said about Demetrius in John's third letter. However there obviously was much said about him through the testimony of others. Why is it significant that those who live for Jesus don't do it for the recognition of others, yet others truly acknowledge and appreciate their lives?

Day Fifty-Six

The Letters of John

Peace Be to You

²⁴ The Lord bless you and keep you;
²⁵ the Lord make his face shine on you
and be gracious to you;
²⁶ the Lord turn his face toward you
and give you peace.
Numbers 6:24-26 (NIV)

Text: 3 John 1:13-15
¹³ I had much to write to you, but I would rather not write with pen and ink. ¹⁴ I hope to see you soon, and we will talk face to face. ¹⁵ Peace be to you. The friends greet you. Greet the friends, each by name.

Thoughts:
John closes out his third letter and hopes to see his fellow believers soon. He lets them know that there is much more that he could have written, but some things are best said in person. John knew the importance of face-to-face conversations and real relationships. He also knew the significance of getting to know someone by name.

David Guzik's words here add great insight into John's closing remarks:

The friends greet you: In addition to a familiar blessing of **peace** upon Gaius, John also reminded him (and us) of the common ties of Christians – even if they are separated by miles, they are still friends in Jesus, and appropriately they should greet one another.

Peace be to you: This is a letter about contention and conflict; yet John appropriately ends the letter with a desire and expectation for peace. As Christians, we can and should have a sense of peace even in the midst of difficult times. Christians have the resources in Jesus Christ to have peace even in unsettled seasons.[1]

James Montgomery Boice adds these words:

The conclusion to 3 John is similar to the verses that end 2 John, except that the author appends a far more personal greeting. "Peace to you. The friends here send their greetings. Greet the friends there by name." The greeting "Peace to you" was adopted by Christians from Hebrew usage, though it was infused with new meaning by Jesus following his resurrection (John 20:19, 21, 26).[2]

Boice's comments remind us that the apostle John had heard Jesus talk about peace. In fact, John had written down what Jesus said so everyone could be reminded of the importance of peace. Notice the following verses:

John 20:19-21, 26 (ESV)
[19] On the evening of that day, the first day of the week, the doors being locked where the disciples were for fear of the Jews, Jesus came and stood among them and said to them, "Peace be with you." [20] When he had said this, he showed them his hands and his side. Then the disciples were glad when

they saw the Lord. [21] Jesus said to them again, "Peace be with you. As the Father has sent me, even so I am sending you."

[26] Eight days later, his disciples were inside again, and Thomas was with them. Although the doors were locked, Jesus came and stood among them and said, "Peace be with you."

As the "Prince of Peace" (Isaiah 9:6), Jesus has divine capability to bring peace to our lives. As He spoke peace to His first disciples, Christ still desires for all of His followers to experience peace. When troubles surround us, Jesus is still the solid rock on which we stand. That's why the peace of God is not the absence of conflict, but the presence of Jesus.

The following story illustrates this truth:

> A ship was wrecked in a furious storm and the only survivor was a little boy who was swept by the waves onto a rock. He sat there all night long until, the next morning, he was spotted and rescued.
>
> "Did you tremble while you were on the rock during the night?" someone later asked him.
>
> "Yes," said the boy. "I trembled all night – but the rock didn't."[3]

As you draw closer to Christ, you will continually find his strength is more than enough for the storms you encounter. We hope you experience his assurance in the midst of uncertainties. We pray that you encounter daily the joy of Jesus and that his peace always fills your heart. As we close out our study, stay close to Jesus. May John's repetitive themes of life, light, and love continually challenge you to live daily in light of eternity and shine your light for Jesus as you love one another.

Questions:

1. How does it make you feel when someone forgets your name? How important is it to greet one another by name?

2. In a world filled with separation and isolation, how can you prioritize relationships with other believers as you grow in your walk with Christ?

3. How would you define the peace of God? In what ways are you experiencing his peace in your life?

4. Vance Havner once said: "Not everyone who has made peace with God has realized the peace of God."[4]

As we conclude our study on the Letters of John, what are your thoughts on Havner's statement?

The Letters of John

Notes

Introduction

[1]Phillips, John. 2009. *Exploring the Epistles of John: An Expository Commentary*. The John Phillips Commentary Series. Kregel Publications; WORDsearch Corp.

[2]Wilkinson, Bruce, and Kenneth Boa. 1983. *Talk Thru the Bible*. Nashville: T. Nelson.

[3]Vaughan, Curtis. 2011. *1, 2, 3 John*. Founders Study Guide Commentary. Cape Coral, FL: Founders Press.

[4]Swindoll, Charles R. 2018. *Insights on 1, 2 & 3 John, Jude*. Vol. 14. Swindoll's Living Insights New Testament Commentary. Carol Stream, IL: Tyndale House Publishers.

Day 1

[1]Anderson, David R. 2013. *Maximum Joy: 1 John – Relationship or Fellowship?* Grace Theology Press.

[2]Ibid.

[3]Ibid.

Day 2

[1]Wellman, P. J. (2015, December 29). *23 quotes about witnessing*. ChristianQuotes.info. https://www.christianquotes.info/quotes-by-topic/quotes-about-witnessing/

[2]Harbour, Brian L. 2013. *Verse by Verse Bible Studies on 1 John*. Notable Harbour Verse Studies. WORDsearch.

Day 3

[1]Davis, O. (2021, January 5). *10 encouraging quotes on biblical joy*. Looking Upward. https://lookingupward.org/2020/04/23/10-encouraging-quotes-on-biblical-joy

[2]Barton, Bruce B., and Grant R. Osborne. 1998. *1, 2 & 3 John*. Life Application Bible Commentary. Wheaton, IL: Tyndale House.

[3]Davis, O. (2021, January 5). *10 encouraging quotes on biblical joy*. Looking Upward. https://lookingupward.org/2020/04/23/10-encouraging-quotes-on-biblical-joy

Day 4

[1]Davis, O. (2021, January 5). *10 encouraging quotes on biblical joy*. Looking Upward. https://lookingupward.org/2020/04/23/10-encouraging-quotes-on-biblical-joy

[2]Barton, Bruce B., and Grant R. Osborne. 1998. *1, 2 & 3 John*. Life Application Bible Commentary. Wheaton, IL: Tyndale House.

[3]Davis, O. (2021, January 5). *10 encouraging quotes on biblical joy*. Looking Upward. https://lookingupward.org/2020/04/23/10-encouraging-quotes-on-biblical-joy

Day 5

[1]Teresa, M. (n.d.). *Top 25 Light of Christ quotes: A-Z quotes*. AZQuotes. https://www.azquotes.com/quotes/topics/Light-of-Christ.html

[2]Aurandt, Paul. 1980. *More of Paul Harvey's The Rest of the Story*. New York, NY: Bantam Books, 1-2.

Day 6

[1]Hoefler, Richard Carl. 1979. *Will Daylight Come?: Background on the Miracles*. Lima, OH: C.S.S. Publishing Co.

Day 7
[1]Phillips, John. 2009. *Exploring the Epistles of John: An Expository Commentary*. The John Phillips Commentary Series. Kregel Publications; WORDsearch Corp.

Day 8
[1]Jackman, David. 1988. *The Message of John's Letters: Living in the Love of God*. The Bible Speaks Today. Leicester, England; Downer's Grove, IL: InterVarsity Press.

Day 9
[1]Piper, J. (2019, December 11). *Jesus_Christ-advocate*. Grace Quotes. https://gracequotes.org/topic/Jesus_Christ-advocate/
[2]Mattoon, Rod. 2017. *Treasures from First … Second … Third John*. Treasures from Scripture Series. Springfield, IL: Rod Mattoon.
[3]Ibid.

Day 10
[1]Packer, J. I. (n.d.). *Top 25 knowing God quotes (of 385): A-Z quotes*. A. https://www.azquotes.com/quotes/topics/knowing-God.html
[2]Hodges, Zane Clark. 1999. *The Epistle of John: Walking in the Light of God's Love*. Irving, TX: Grace Evangelical Society.
[3]Ibid.

Day 11
[1]Eldredge, J. (n.d.). *Top 25 walking with God quotes (of 70): A-Z quotes*. A. https://www.azquotes.com/quotes/topics/walking-with-God.html
[2]Barton, Bruce B., and Grant R. Osborne. 1998. *1, 2 & 3 John*. Life Application Bible Commentary. Wheaton, IL: Tyndale House.
[3]Lutzer, E. (n.d.). *Top 25 walking with God quotes (of 70): A-Z quotes*. A. https://www.azquotes.com/quotes/topics/walking-with-God.html

Day 12

[1]Piper, J. (n.d.). Commandment quotes - brainyquote. https://www.brainyquote.com/topics/commandment-quotes

[2]Walls, David, and Max Anders. 1999. *Holman New Testament Commentary: 1 & 2 Peter, 1, 2, & 3 John, Jude*. Nashville, TN: Broadman and Holman Publishers.

Day 13

[1]Fonseca, E. (2019, June 17). *25 beautiful quotes about God's love*. The Scribe's Portion. https://www.thescribesportion.com/beautiful-quotes-Gods-love/

[2]Ibid.

[3]Ibid.

Day 14

[1]Packer, B. (n.d.). *Top 25 child of God quotes (of 277): A-Z quotes*. A. https://www.azquotes.com/quotes/topics/child-of-God.html

[2]Lucado, M. (n.d.). *Top 25 child of God quotes (of 277): A-Z quotes*. A. https://www.azquotes.com/quotes/topics/child-of-God.html

Day 15

[1]Allen, David L. 2013. *1–3 John: Fellowship in God's Family*. Edited by R. Kent Hughes. Preaching the Word. Wheaton, IL: Crossway.

[2]Ibid.

Day 16

[1]Wellman, P. J. (2015, December 22). *77 quotes about Eternity*. ChristianQuotes.info. https://www.christianquotes.info/quotes-by-topic/quotes-about-eternity/

[2]Ibid.

[3]Ibid.

[4]Ibid.

Day 17

[1]Cole, Steven J. 2017. "Lesson 10: Avoiding Spiritual Deception, Part 1 (1 John 2:18–23)." In *1 John*, 1 Jn 2:18–23. Steven J. Cole Commentary Series. Dallas: Galaxie Software.

[2]Case, David A., and David W. Holdren. 2006. *1-2 Peter, 1-3 John, Jude: A Commentary for Bible Students*. Indianapolis, IN: Wesleyan Publishing House.

[3]Ibid.

[4]Ibid.

Day 18

[1]Swindoll, Charles R. 2018. *Insights on 1, 2 & 3 John, Jude*. Vol. 14. Swindoll's Living Insights New Testament Commentary. Carol Stream, IL: Tyndale House Publishers.

[2]Ibid.

[3]Jackman, David. 1988. *The Message of John's Letters: Living in the Love of God*. The Bible Speaks Today. Leicester, England; Downer's Grove, IL: InterVarsity Press.

Day 19

[1]Mattoon, Rod. 2017. *Treasures from First … Second … Third John*. Treasures from Scripture Series. Springfield, IL: Rod Mattoon.

[2]Barton, Bruce B., and Grant R. Osborne. 1998. *1, 2 & 3 John*. Life Application Bible Commentary. Wheaton, IL: Tyndale House.

[3]Ibid.

Day 20

[1]Ryle, J. C. (n.d.). *Abiding in Christ*. J.C. Ryle Quotes. https://www.rylequotes.org/quotes/abiding-in-Christ6319134

[2]*Listening Sermon Illustrations*. sermonillustrations.com. (n.d.). https://www.sermonillustrations.com/a-z/l/listening.htm

[3]Ibid.

⁴Gonzales, N. (2019, August 28). *8 favorite quotes from the book "Abide" by Warren W. Wiersbe*. Delighting Grace. https://delightinggrace.wordpress.com/2019/08/21/8-favorite-quotes-from-the-book-abide-by-warren-w-wiersbe/

Day 21
¹Conrad, M. R. (2022, May 24). *Missionary quotes about abiding in Christ*. Rooted Thinking. https://rootedthinking.com/2022/05/26/missionary-quotes-about-abiding-in-Christ/

²Taylor, Dr. and Mrs. Howard. 1918. *Hudson Taylor and the China Inland Mission: The Growth of a Work of God*. Singapore: OMF International, 173–177.

Day 22
¹Tozer, A. W. (n.d.-a). *Preparing for Jesus' return quotes*. Goodreads. https://www.goodreads.com/work/quotes/18940727-preparing-for-Jesus-return-daily-live-the-blessed-hope
²Tozer. A.W. 2012. *Whatever Happened to Worship: A Call to True Worship*. Camp Hill, PA: Wingspread Publishers.

Day 23
¹Hunt, B. (2019, May 24). *11 quotes on the Miracle of New Birth*. St. George's Anglican Church. https://www.stgeorgesonline.com/2019/05/23/11-quotes-on-the-miracle-of-new-birth/
²Ibid.
³Sproul, R. C. (n.d.). *Top 25 righteousness quotes*: azquotes.com. https://www.azquotes.com/quotes/topics/righteousness.html

Day 24
¹Green, Michael P., ed. 1989. *Illustrations for Biblical Preaching: Over 1500 Sermon Illustrations Arranged by Topic and Indexed Exhaustively*. Revised edition of: The expositor's illustration file. Grand Rapids: Baker Book House.

[2]Jeremiah, David. 2012. *God Loves You: He Always Has--He Always Will*. New York City, NY: FaithWords.
[3]Chery, F. (2024, January 15). *100 inspirational quotes about God's love for Us*. Bible Reasons | Bible Verses About Various Topics. https://biblereasons.com/Gods-love-quotes/
[4]Ibid.
[5]Ibid.

Day 25
[1]Graham, Bi. (n.d.). *Face to face quotes.* azquotes.com. https://www.azquotes.com/quotes/topics/face-to-face.html?p=3
[2]Barton, Bruce B., and Grant R. Osborne. 1998. *1, 2 & 3 John*. Life Application Bible Commentary. Wheaton, IL: Tyndale House.
[3]Allen, David L. 2013. *1–3 John: Fellowship in God's Family*. Edited by R. Kent Hughes. Preaching the Word. Wheaton, IL: Crossway.

Day 26
[1]Keller, T. (2022, April 8). *Top 15 inspirational Christian hope quotes*. Our God is With Us. https://www.ourgodiswithus.com/top-15-inspirational-Christian-hope-quotes/
[2]Case, David A., and David W. Holdren. 2006. *1-2 Peter, 1-3 John, Jude: A Commentary for Bible Students*. Indianapolis, IN: Wesleyan Publishing House.

Day 27
[1]Rogers, A. (n.d.). *Adrian Rogers quote.* Quotefancy. https://quotefancy.com/quote/1528089/
[2]Case, David A., and David W. Holdren. 2006. *1-2 Peter, 1-3 John, Jude: A Commentary for Bible Students*. Indianapolis, IN: Wesleyan Publishing House.

Day 28

[1]DeYoung, K. (n.d.). *Top 25 child of God quotes (of 277): A-Z quotes*. azquotes.com. https://www.azquotes.com/quotes/topics/child-of-god.html

[2]Stott, J. (n.d.). *Top 25 child of God quotes (of 277): A-Z quotes*. azquotes.com. https://www.azquotes.com/quotes/topics/child-of-god.html

[3] Allen, David L. 2013. *1–3 John: Fellowship in God's Family*. Edited by R. Kent Hughes. Preaching the Word. Wheaton, IL: Crossway.

Day 29

[1]Rowell, Edward, ed. 2008. *1001 Quotes, Illustrations, and Humorous Stories: For Preachers, Teachers and Writers*. Baker Publishing Group.

[2]Allen, David L. 2013. *1–3 John: Fellowship in God's Family*. Edited by R. Kent Hughes. Preaching the Word. Wheaton, IL: Crossway.

[3]Cole, Steven J. 2017. "Lesson 16: Hatred or Love? (1 John 3:11–18)." In *1 John*, 1 Jn 3:11–18. Steven J. Cole Commentary Series. Dallas: Galaxie Software.

Day 30

[1] Stott, J. (2019, December 11). *Love-OTHERS_FOR*. Grace Quotes. https://gracequotes.org/topic/love-others_for/

[2]Cole, Steven J. 2017. "Lesson 16: Hatred or Love? (1 John 3:11–18)." In *1 John*, 1 Jn 3:11–18. Steven J. Cole Commentary Series. Dallas: Galaxie Software.

Day 31

[1]Wesley, J. (n.d.). *John Wesley Quotes (author of a plain account of Christian perfection)*. Goodreads. https://www.goodreads.com/author/quotes/151350.John_Wesley

[2]Mattoon, Rod. 2017. *Treasures from First … Second … Third John*. Treasures from Scripture Series. Springfield, IL: Rod Mattoon.

Day 32

[1]Rowell, Edward, ed. 2008. *1001 Quotes, Illustrations, and Humorous Stories: For Preachers, Teachers and Writers*. Baker Publishing Group.

[2]Case, David A., and David W. Holdren. 2006. *1-2 Peter, 1-3 John, Jude: A Commentary for Bible Students*. Indianapolis, IN: Wesleyan Publishing House.

[3]Barton, Bruce B., and Grant R. Osborne. 1998. *1, 2 & 3 John*. Life Application Bible Commentary. Wheaton, IL: Tyndale House.

Day 33

[1]Luther, M. (n.d.). *Top 25 faith in love quotes: A-Z quotes*. A. https://www.azquotes.com/quotes/topics/faith-in-love.html

Day 34

[1]Guzik, David. 2013. *1 John*. David Guzik's Commentaries on the Bible. Santa Barbara, CA: David Guzik.

[2]Vaughan, Curtis. 2011. *1, 2, 3 John*. Founders Study Guide Commentary. Cape Coral, FL: Founders Press.

Day 35

[1]Wright, N. T. (n.d.). *Top 25 greatness of God quotes (of 189): A-Z quotes*. A. https://www.azquotes.com/quotes/topics/greatness-of-god.html

[2] Sproul, R. C. (n.d.). *Top 25 greatness of God quotes (of 189): A-Z quotes*. A. https://www.azquotes.com/quotes/topics/greatness-of-god.html

[3]Case, David A., and David W. Holdren. 2006. *1-2 Peter, 1-3 John, Jude: A Commentary for Bible Students*. Indianapolis, IN: Wesleyan Publishing House.

[4]Barton, Bruce B., and Grant R. Osborne. 1998. *1, 2 & 3 John*. Life Application Bible Commentary. Wheaton, IL: Tyndale House.

[5]Stott, John R. W. 1988. *The Letters of John: An Introduction and Commentary*. Vol. 19. Tyndale New Testament Commentaries. Downers Grove, IL: InterVarsity Press.

Day 36

[1]Dunnam, M. (2023, April 8). *A Christian is hopelessly in love with Jesus and helplessly dependent on Him*. Maxie Dunnam. https://maxiedunnam.com/category/maxies-quotes/

[2]Allen, David L. 2013. *1–3 John: Fellowship in God's Family*. Edited by R. Kent Hughes. Preaching the Word. Wheaton, IL: Crossway.

[3]Cole, Steven J. 2017. "Lesson 19: Why We Must Love (1 John 4:7–11)." In *1 John*, 1 Jn 4:7–11. Steven J. Cole Commentary Series. Dallas: Galaxie Software.

[4]Case, David A., and David W. Holdren. 2006. *1-2 Peter, 1-3 John, Jude: A Commentary for Bible Students*. Indianapolis, IN: Wesleyan Publishing House.

[5]Allen, David L. 2013. *1–3 John: Fellowship in God's Family*. Edited by R. Kent Hughes. Preaching the Word. Wheaton, IL: Crossway.

[6]Ibid.

Day 37

[1]Augustine, St. (2023, February 8). *15 amazing quotes about god's love*. Guideposts. https://guideposts.org/daily-devotions/10-amazing-quotes-about-gods-love/

[2] Spurgeon, C. (2024b, January 15). *100 inspirational quotes about God's love for Us*. biblereasons.com. https://biblereasons.com/gods-love-quotes/

[3] Witherington, B. (1970, January 1). *The Nature of True love*. http://benwitherington.blogspot.com/2009/01/nature-of-true-love.html

Day 38

[1]Stott, John R. W. 1988. *The Letters of John: An Introduction and Commentary*. Vol. 19. Tyndale New Testament Commentaries. Downers Grove, IL: InterVarsity Press.

[2]Williamson, Rick. 2010. *1, 2, & 3 John: A Commentary in the Wesleyan Tradition*. New Beacon Bible Commentary. Kansas City, MO: Beacon Hill Press.

Day 39

[1]Guzik, David. 2013. *1 John*. David Guzik's Commentaries on the Bible. Santa Barbara, CA: David Guzik.
[2]Ibid.
[3]Evans, Tony. 2009. *Tony Evans' Book of Illustrations: Stories, Quotes, and Anecdotes from More than 30 Years of Preaching and Public Speaking*. Chicago, IL: Moody Publishers.

Day 40

[1]Bridges, J. (2019, December 11). *Love-OTHERS_FOR*. Grace Quotes. https://gracequotes.org/topic/love-others_for/
[2]Case, David A., and David W. Holdren. 2006. *1-2 Peter, 1-3 John, Jude: A Commentary for Bible Students*. Indianapolis, IN: Wesleyan Publishing House.
[3]Witherington, B. (1970, January 1). *The Nature of True love*. http://benwitherington.blogspot.com/2009/01/nature-of-true-love.html
[4]Ibid.

Day 41

[1]PreachingToday.com. 2002. *Perfect Illustrations: For Every Topic and Occasion*. Wheaton, IL: Tyndale House Publishers, Inc.

Day 42

[1]Morgan, Robert J. 2000. *Nelson's Complete Book of Stories, Illustrations, and Quotes*. Electronic ed. Nashville: Thomas Nelson Publishers.
[2]Mattoon, Rod. 2017. *Treasures from First … Second … Third John*. Treasures from Scripture Series. Springfield, IL: Rod Mattoon.
[3]Morgan, Robert J. 2010. *Near to the Heart of God: Meditations on 366 Best-Loved Hymns*. Grand Rapids, MI: Revell.

Day 44

[1]Guzik, David. 2013. *1 John*. David Guzik's Commentaries on the Bible. Santa Barbara, CA: David Guzik.

[2]Barton, Bruce B., and Grant R. Osborne. 1998. *1, 2 & 3 John*. Life Application Bible Commentary. Wheaton, IL: Tyndale House.

[3]Allen, David L. 2013. *1–3 John: Fellowship in God's Family*. Edited by R. Kent Hughes. Preaching the Word. Wheaton, IL: Crossway.

Day 45

[1]Case, David A., and David W. Holdren. 2006. *1-2 Peter, 1-3 John, Jude: A Commentary for Bible Students*. Indianapolis, IN: Wesleyan Publishing House.

[2]Akin, Daniel L. 2014. *Exalting Jesus in 1,2,3 John*. Nashville, TN: Holman Reference.

[3] Strauss, Lehman. 1971. *The Epistles of John: Devotional Studies on John's Three Letters*. Horizon Press.

Day 46

[1]Wiersbe, Warren W. 1996. *The Bible Exposition Commentary*. Vol. 2. Wheaton, IL: Victor Books.

[2]Ibid.

[3]Harbour, Brian L. 2013. *Verse by Verse Bible Studies on 1 John*. Notable Harbour Verse Studies. WORDsearch.

[4]Guzik, David. 2013. *1 John*. David Guzik's Commentaries on the Bible. Santa Barbara, CA: David Guzik.

[5]Wiersbe, Warren W. 1996. *The Bible Exposition Commentary*. Vol. 2. Wheaton, IL: Victor Books.

Day 47

[1] Edwards, J. (n.d.). *Top 25 sin quotes (of 1000): A-Z quotes*. A. https://www.azquotes.com/quotes/topics/sin.html

[2] Williamson, Rick. 2010. *1, 2, & 3 John: A Commentary in the Wesleyan Tradition*. New Beacon Bible Commentary. Kansas City, MO: Beacon Hill Press.

[3]Spurgeon, C. (n.d.). *Battle for the Truth*. Charles Spurgeon and the Battle For Truth. https://www.wayoflife.org/reports/charles-spurgeon-and-the-battle-for-truth.php

[4]Akin, Daniel L. 2001. *1, 2, 3 John*. Vol. 38. The New American Commentary. Nashville: Broadman & Holman Publishers.

Day 48

[1] Schaeffer, F. (2015, December 29). *212 quotes about truth*. ChristianQuotes.info. https://www.christianquotes.info/quotes-by-topic/quotes-about-truth/

[2]Allen, David L. 2013. *1–3 John: Fellowship in God's Family*. Edited by R. Kent Hughes. Preaching the Word. Wheaton, IL: Crossway.

Day 49

[1] Spurgeon, C. *Top 25 idolatry quotes:* azquotes.com. https://www.azquotes.com/quotes/topics/idolatry.html

[2]Guzik, David. 2013. *1 John*. David Guzik's Commentaries on the Bible. Santa Barbara, CA: David Guzik.

[3]Wiersbe, Warren W. 1996. *The Bible Exposition Commentary*. Vol. 2. Wheaton, IL: Victor Books.

Day 50

[1]Cole, Steven J. 2017. "Lesson 1: Rx for a Healthy Church, Part 1 (2 John 1–6)." In *2 John*, 2 Jn 1–6. Steven J. Cole Commentary Series. Dallas: Galaxie Software.

[2]Barton, Bruce B., and Grant R. Osborne. 1998. *1, 2 & 3 John*. Life Application Bible Commentary. Wheaton, IL: Tyndale House.

[3]Cole, Steven J. 2017. "Lesson 1: Rx for a Healthy Church, Part 1 (2 John 1–6)." In *2 John*, 2 Jn 1–6. Steven J. Cole Commentary Series. Dallas: Galaxie Software.

Day 51

[1]Swindoll, Charles R. 2018. *Insights on 1, 2 & 3 John, Jude*. Vol. 14. Swindoll's Living Insights New Testament Commentary. Carol Stream, IL: Tyndale House Publishers.

[2] Case, David A., and David W. Holdren. 2006. *1-2 Peter, 1-3 John, Jude: A Commentary for Bible Students*. Indianapolis, IN: Wesleyan Publishing House.

Day 52

[1]Begg, A. (n.d.). *Top 25 relationship with God quotes (of 201):* azquotes. com. https://www.azquotes.com/quotes/topics/relationship-with-god.html

[2]Moore, B. (2022, July 7). *Isolation archives*. Daily Christian Quotes. https://www.dailychristianquote.com/tag/isolation/

[3]Swindoll, Charles R. 2018. *Insights on 1, 2 & 3 John, Jude*. Vol. 14. Swindoll's Living Insights New Testament Commentary. Carol Stream, IL: Tyndale House Publishers.

Day 53

[1] Bailey, B. (2016, November 18). *No greater joy*. Wisdom Hunters. https://www.wisdomhunters.com/no-greater-joy-2/

[2] Allen, David L. 2013. *1–3 John: Fellowship in God's Family*. Edited by R. Kent Hughes. Preaching the Word. Wheaton, IL: Crossway.

[3] Barton, Bruce B., and Grant R. Osborne. 1998. *1, 2 & 3 John*. Life Application Bible Commentary. Wheaton, IL: Tyndale House.

Day 54

[1]MacLaren, A. (2022, February 17). *Fellow-workers with the truth (3 John 1:8) by Alexander Maclaren*. Blue Letter Bible. https://www.blueletterbible.org/comm/maclaren_alexander/expositions-of-holy-scripture/3-john/fellow-workers-with-the-truth.cfm

[2]Morgan, Robert J. 2000. *Nelson's Complete Book of Stories, Illustrations, and Quotes*. Electronic ed. Nashville: Thomas Nelson Publishers.

Day 55

[1]Allen, David L. 2013. *1–3 John: Fellowship in God's Family*. Edited by R. Kent Hughes. Preaching the Word. Wheaton, IL: Crossway.

[2] Case, David A., and David W. Holdren. 2006. *1-2 Peter, 1-3 John, Jude: A Commentary for Bible Students*. Indianapolis, IN: Wesleyan Publishing House.

[3] Swindoll, Charles R. 2018. *Insights on 1, 2 & 3 John, Jude*. Vol. 14. Swindoll's Living Insights New Testament Commentary. Carol Stream, IL: Tyndale House Publishers.

Day 56

[1]Guzik, David. 2013. *3 John*. David Guzik's Commentaries on the Bible. Santa Barbara, CA: David Guzik.

[2]Boice, James Montgomery. 2004. *The Epistles of John: An Expositional Commentary*. Grand Rapids, MI: Baker Books.

[3]Morgan, Robert J. 2000. *Nelson's Complete Book of Stories, Illustrations, and Quotes*. Electronic ed. Nashville: Thomas Nelson Publishers.

[4]Havner, V. (n.d.). *Top 25 peace with God quotes: A-Z quotes*. azquotes. com. https://www.azquotes.com/quotes/topics/peace-with-god. html

Made in the USA
Columbia, SC
22 November 2024

46790765R00130